Spanish Cooking

Spanish Cooking

A Fiesta of Original Regional Recipes

PEPITA ARIS

CHARTWELL
BOOKS, INC.

A   QUINTET   BOOK

Published by Chartwell Books
A Division of Book Sales, Inc.
110 Enterprise Avenue
Secaucus, New Jersey 07094

This edition produced for sale
in the U.S.A., its territories
and dependencies only.

ISBN 1–55521–928–4

This book was designed and produced by
Quintet Publishing Limited
6 Blundell Street
London N7 9BH

Creative Director: Richard Dewing
Designer: Ian Hunt
Project Editor: Helen Denholm
Editor: Michelle Clarke
Food Photographer: Nelson Hargreaves
Photographic Stylist: Pamela Westland

With thanks to the following photographers for
providing general pictures of Spain:

Pierre Coulon: pages 2, 8 (above), 10 (above), 11,
26, 31, 34, 42, 56, 68, 74, 76, 82, 86, 96, 98, 103, 120

Peter Wilson: pages 6, 7, 8 (below), 9 (above and
below), 10 (below), 12, 13, 14, 24, 46, 54, 106, 108

Typeset in Great Britain by
Central Southern Typesetters, Eastbourne
Manufactured in Singapore by Eray Scan Pte. Ltd.
Printed in Singapore by Star Standard Pte. Ltd.

Contents

The Regions of Spain 6

CHAPTER 1   Andalusia 14

CHAPTER 2   Extremadura 26

CHAPTER 3   New Castile and La Mancha 34

CHAPTER 4   Old Castile 46

CHAPTER 5   Galicia 56

CHAPTER 6   Asturias and Cantabria 68

CHAPTER 7   The Basque Country 76

CHAPTER 8   Navarre and Aragon 86

CHAPTER 9   Catalonia 96

CHAPTER 10 Levante 108

CHAPTER 11 The Balearic Islands 120

Index 128

The Regions of Spain

*S*pain has a greater geographical variety than any other
European country. Though its borders are clearly defined,
it has been one country for less than 500 years. For these
reasons each region is more conscious of its separate
identity than of its Spanish nationality. Food is one way in
which the regions express their local individuality.

Two themes run through the cooking of almost the whole country. The Moors, who stayed for nearly 1000 years, gave Spain its first taste of civilized life, with a remarkable cuisine that still survives. The struggle to throw out the infidels brought a second big influence to Spain's cuisine. Spain united behind the pig, for neither Moor nor Jew ate pork, and pork cookery became almost part of the Christian religion.

A third common idea is part of Spanish good sense and good taste. Respect for, and interest in, splendid ingredients is universal. Recipes may seem simple, but they are very well judged to show off food of excellent quality without unnecessary complications. The result is a cuisine that is straightforward, but extremely tasty.

The South and West

Every image that is Spain comes from Andalusia: orange trees and the tinkling jug of icy *sangría*; flamenco and bullfighting; the brown sierras with whitewashed villages clinging to their sides. It is the huge underbelly of Spain – one-sixth of the country. It embraces the Atlantic coast, the high mountains centered on Granada (snowy all year round) and the deserts of Almería (which have recently begun to bloom under plastic). Some of the best-known sunshine tourist beaches are here too, on Europe's warmest shore.

The Moors made their mark on the landscape by planting olive and orange trees. Their influence on the cuisine is clear: spices like cumin and saffron, the use of nuts, all ground with mortar and pestle, a taste for frying in olive oil. Chilled soups, barbecued skewered meat, their way of pickling fish, little almond sweetmeats and *membrillo* (a stiff quince paste) are still common.

Tapas were invented here: morsels of food accompanying drinks, such as olives, salted almonds or dark red, raw ham with bread. Complete with trotters, these hams hang over all the bars. They are cured in the cold air of the sierras, which gives them the name *serrano*. Jabugo ham is the best known.

The Costa del Sol is well known for its fried fish. Cadiz makes a mixture called *pescaito frito* and every beach-bar on the coast sells the popular battered squid rings called *calamares*. There are also excellent fish soups, tiny deep-fried fish called *chanquetes*, stews of shark, skate cooked with paprika and broiled swordfish steaks.

Jerez, from which we derive our word sherry, makes a dry, pale *fino* that is one of the world's great white wines. Here it is drunk chilled with fish. In the kitchen it provides the sauce for the bull's tail, kidneys or delicate combinations of veal.

The bullring at Ronda in Andalusia, the home of bullfighting.

Seville is famous for introducing oranges to Europe – "duck with orange" was invented here – then, much later, tomatoes and peppers from America. All go into local dishes. Andalusia has also learned much from the gypsies. Their popular dish is *huevos flamencos*, a colorful mixture of eggs, peppers, shrimp and/or sausage. There are gypsy stews which use beans, vegetables and fruit, and good dishes of tripe with sausage and garbanzo beans.

To the north of Andalusia, in the west of Spain, parallel to the Portuguese border, is Extremadura. Its name means "extreme and hard" but, in fact, it has some of Spain's most beautiful rolling countryside. Sheep and pigs graze under cork oaks and the evergreen holm oak. Lamb is the luxury, fried or made into a stew with its own liver – *calderete extremeño*.

Many of Spain's great explorers like Pizarro and Cortes started life here in this poor region and left, as others do now, to seek their fortune. The dishes are modest, though served in generous quantities. Fried breadcrumbs, called *migas*, vegetable soups, and dishes based on tomatoes or offal are the basic food of the region. The hams are well known; the sausages splendid.

Wild food is a specialty, including frogs' legs and tench in autumn, game birds of all sorts, and even lizard. Europe's most luxurious pheasant dish was invented here in the monastery of Alcántara, but the monks no longer eat it.

A decorative mirador window in Trujillo.

Wall tiles from the Plaza de España in Seville, depicting Leon,
a kingdom in the north of Spain.

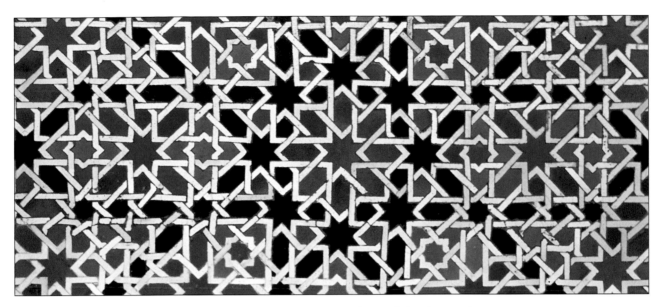

Tiles from the Alcázar in Seville. The use of white lines in the pattern is typical of Moorish design.

Central Spain

A huge, high plateau, Castile dominates the center of Spain. Madrid is here – chosen only 400 years ago as the capital because it is at the center of the country.

To its south is New Castile and La Mancha. This is Don Quixote and windmill country – an open plain, bitterly cold in winter, yet gasping under a burning sky in summer. Food is simple: meatballs, garbanzo beans, and *pisto manchego*, vegetables simmered with tomatoes. Tortilla was invented here.

The hard climate has bred strong, raw, tastes. Garlic soups are popular and local dishes are notable for including thyme and cumin. The latter was introduced by the Arabs when they planted saffron. Castile now grows the finest saffron in the world. Game birds provide occasional meat, and partridges are cooked with wine and vinegar or made into game pâtés like *gazpacho manchego*.

Cut off from Madrid by the Guadarrama mountains, Old Castile runs northwards to the mountains behind the coast. Many sheep graze here and their milk goes to make the country's most distinguished cheese, Manchego.

Old Castile is a land of castles and the *zona de asados*, where roasts are prepared in the old beehive Arab ovens. Sepúlveda is celebrated for its suckling lamb and Arévolo for its tiny roast piglets. Poorer families, however, eat beans, lentils and garbanzo beans, as in the

A statue of the Virgin and Child in the cathedral of San Isidro, in Madrid. San Isidro is the city's patron saint.

A narrow street with whitewashed buildings in San Roque.

excellent *garbanzos con chorizos*, which includes red sausage. Old Castile is also Spain's bread basket, growing fine wheat used to make the large, round, white loaves.

So vast an area embraces many individual regions. The old kingdom of León, in the western corner, is backed by mountains and is known for its game, trout,

A tiled advertisement for a tapas bar.

and bean dishes. At the opposite corner of Castile (due south of the Basque country) is Rioja. This is the region of Spain's best red-wine vineyards, and it also grows wonderful peppers. *Patatas a la riojana*, for example, are potatoes flavored with paprika, or with delicious paprika sausage.

Madrid itself is home to all styles of cooking and is full of good, authentic regional restaurants. Its night life and *tapas* bars are famous. The city-dwellers like good meat – huge steaks and milk-fed veal from Avila. Dishes with the adjective *madrileño* are from the old days; like *cocido*, the pot of simmered meats and tripe stewed with pork pieces.

In Old Castile there is a tradition of little cakes, often made by nuns who earn income from them. The yellow egg yolk *yemas* of Avila are famous.

The North Coast

Buffeted by the scouring, roaring Atlantic, the northern coast of Spain has little in common with the tourist beaches of the south. This is Spain's "Celtic fringe," more like a warmer version of Wales than Spain. The countryside is misty and green and Galicia grows cabbages, turnips, potatoes and lettuces for the whole of Spain.

At Spain's western corner, the countryside is studded with little *horreos*, sheds on stilts used to store maize and cheeses. The Atlantic wind blows and blows, so, to keep it out, there are powerful drinks like *queimada*, which is the local *eau-de-vie*, *aguardiente*, set on fire.

Here they make some of the best fish stews in the world. This is not because the cooking is sophisticated – it is extremely plain – but because they have the freshest fish in Europe, caught in the fastest-moving water.

The seafood is famous: octopus, oysters, huge orange mussels, and the scallops, which are the badge of pilgrims to the shrine of St James at Santiago. There are splendid rock lobsters and strange, costly, tubular black barnacles called *percebes*.

Galicia differs from the rest of Spain in all sorts of ways, for example in its unique flat pies, called *empanadas*. They often contain shellfish, the excellent local sardines, or pork with peppers. This is also the only part of Spain to make rye and corn bread. Cooking is done with pork fat; local recipes rarely include olive oil or garlic. Among the best-known dishes are broths with cabbage, like *caldo gallego*, and *lacón con grelos*, a ham knuckle cooked with young turnip tops.

Some specialties of the area are known across Spain, such as the almond tart that is made to celebrate St James's Day and capons that are fattened for Christmas. Tiny Padrón peppers are grown here, which are deep-fried and then eaten 20 at a time.

Chestnut trees clothe the hillier south of Galicia, where the living is poorer. The chestnuts are eaten as potatoes are elsewhere. They also make superb sugary *marrons glacés*, which Alexander Dumas thought the best in the world.

Running parallel to the north coast is a 300-mile mountain range, rising to 8000ft in places. It butts into Galicia, forms the "eyebrow" round León to the west, and the "chin" below Santander to the east. It cuts off the maritime part of Old Castile, to make Cantabria. Asturias is its middle section. It is one of Europe's wildest parts, with pigeon and partridge, red deer, and plenty of trout and salmon. Ironically, Asturias is also Spain's mining region.

It is this background that has created the region's most famous dish. For this is sausage country, home of the smoked, black *morcilla*, that goes into Asturias' flat bean dish, *fabada*.

Asturias also has the best milk in Spain, made into the creamy blue *cabrales* cheese. There is a tradition of milk puddings, for rice first traveled outside the Mediterranean area as a sweet dish. More than 250 varieties of apples blossom and fruit on the mountains' northern side, and the coast is known for apple pies and the fizzy, potent cider that quickly goes flat.

The Cantabrian coast is the corridor of the northern coast, from the Basque country to the west. Many Spanish families holiday here, eating the local clams or baby sardines in sauces and simple dishes named after the surrounding countryside. The city of Santander (like once-royal Brighton) has fine cooking, which echoes that of the Basque country.

The Basque country forms only a tiny triangle of Spain, but it is the most assertive of Spain's provinces. Snuggled next to the Bay of Biscay and the mountains that lead to France, its cooking traditions are different too. Self-styled "gourmets," the Basques have long provided chefs for the rest of Spain. Basques have traditionally looked outwards. There are French-style dishes such as the soft, un-Spanish omelette, *piperrada*. The Basques are also the Atlantic fishermen. The white bonito tuna, and their fish dishes like *marmitako* stew, are famous. Spain's main debt to the Basques, however, is cod, which is salted to make *bacalao*. It is both a Basque and a national passion. Locally it is cooked in a dried pepper sauce, or, *al pil-pil*, in a white emulsion

Hillside villages with stepped streets are dotted all over Spain.

The roofline of the famous Casa Batlló in Barcelona by Antoni Gaudí.

made from the fish's own gelatin.

There are also delicate dishes like hake in green parsley sauce, *merluza en salsa verde*, and exquisite fried sole. Other luxuries are *txangurro* (stuffed crab), *angulas* (thread-like elvers), and *kokotxas*, which are cut from the hake's throat. Their cooking is supervised by the *cofradías*, clubs where men (only) meet to cook. Line-caught squid, cooked in their own ink, are a specialty of Basque *nouvelle cuisine*.

The lucky Basques have all the other things too: dairy products, vegetables, fine meat and game, and mushrooms from the mountains. Chocolate is another local passion.

Pyrenean Spain

The western Pyrenees and its foothills form Navarre, a much-traveled area; the pilgrims to Santiago de Compostello came through here in the old days. Fine lambs are reared in the mountains. They are broiled as tiny chops, roasted or made into *cochifrito* or the stew called *chilindrón*, with dried local peppers.

Navarre has its head in the hills, but its feet down in the warm Ebro valley, where there are vineyards and vegetable gardens. Tudela is famous for its asparagus (made into *tortillas*) and Lodoso for pointed, spicy, red peppers, *pimientos del pico*, which are stuffed with meat or salt cod.

Mountain streams mean trout, and these are cooked in wine or fried in ham fat, and served stuffed or wrapped in ham. Wild rabbits are stewed with snails and with local herbs; partridges and pigeons are netted as they fly over the high mountain passes. Quails cooked with fresh kidney beans, and pigeons in raisin and pinenut sauce are other local specialties.

Aragon is large, dusty and infinitely poorer than Navarre. Spaniards make the same sort of jokes about the locals (and their food) as the British make about the Irish. They do have, though, excellent pork products – sliced ham in tomato sauce is a delicious local dish – and good broiled meats. There are also famous old dishes like the salt cod *bacalao al ajoarriero*, flavored with garlic, parsley, and dried red peppers.

All along the Pyrenees, into Catalonia, there are great fruit orchards, miles of apples and peaches in season, and splendid melons called *piel de sapo*.

The East Coast

Catalonia embraces the Pyrenees (and a chunk of the French border) and the Costa Brava. Its capital, Barcelona, has been a city for good eating for over 150 years. Some of the Mediterranean's best fish stews are found here, like *zarzuela* and *suquet*, gorgeous ebullient combinations of fish and shellfish. There are some wonderful, crazy mixtures like lobster with chicken, or lobster in chocolate sauce. Ducks are cooked with figs, goslings with pears.

There are also celebrated sauces. *Romesco* is one, a toasted hazelnut and chili mix that is delicious with broiled seafood. Another is the glossy, pungent garlic *allioli* – invented here and copied elsewhere.

Barbecues give food a special taste and, unusually, vegetables are barbecued here too. There are *calçots* (a fat green onion) and a mixed broiled vegetable salad with eggplant, called *ecalivada*.

In Catalonia all meals come with tomato-coated bread, the *pa amb tomàquet*. The common food is a fat, fresh, white sausage called *butifarra*, eaten with beans and in stews. Catalans have their own simmered meat pot, too, called *escudella*. They are the most vigorous of mushroom hunters; the pursuit of the golden lactarius, *rovelló*, is a passion. Pasta is popular, particularly *cannelonis* and the local thin *fideos* with seafood. There is also the odd French-influenced dish, like *pollo al villaroy* – chicken breasts coated in white sauce.

Creamy desserts are popular: simple ones, like curds with honey (*mel i mato*), and *crema Catalana*, the local *crème brûlée*. At festival time there are small nut cakes, chiefly *panellets*, and everything is washed down with some of Spain's best white wine and the champagne-style fizz called *cava*.

Levante, "where the east wind blows," takes in most of the east coast, from Cartagena going north. It includes Alicante, Valencia – with its celebrated orange groves – and Murcia, the last Moorish kingdom of Spain, as well as a good many sunshine beaches.

The Arabs cultivated rice here and Murcia and Valencia have scores of saffron rice dishes, including *el caldero* and *arroz a banda*. In both, the rice is cooked in a rich fish broth and served with *allioli*. *Paella* itself was originally a picnic dish, and is less than 200 years old. The rice fields are also well known for eels, cooked *all i pebre*, with garlic and paprika.

Highly-flavored fish and shellfish come from the Mar Menor, an inland sea with a high salt content. The most famous dish is bass or grey mullet, cooked in a jacket of raw salt. Salt also makes the cured *mojama*, from the tuna's back.

Gardens that were once Arab produce wonderful vegetables, oranges, figs, muscat grapes, and dates (the date palms punctuate the skyline round Alicante). The milky summer drink called *horchata* is still made, by grinding an underground tuber called a *chufa*. And Jijona is famous for *turrón*, made from toasted almonds and honey.

Off the eastern coast, the Balearic Islands have been swept over by every civilization. Olive and almond trees grow here, and wild capers and herbs, which influence the cooking. Mallorca has long been a center for sophisticated holidays and yachting. Ibiza was the Med's first hippy colony, while the naval station on Menorca was, in turn, occupied by the English and the French for over a century. The English left gin behind as a "thank you," and it is drunk seriously strong, *en pallofa*. The French found *mahonesa* there at Mahón in the 1770s – and took it home as a French invention!

There are other brilliant creations. *Ensaimada* – probably Arab in origin – is the Mediterranean's best flaky pastry. And *sobrasada* is an exquisite paprika sausage, with a texture reminiscent of *foie gras*. Otherwise the local fare is fresh fish, including excellent rock lobster, *llangosta*, cooked with one of many herb flavored spirits, or solid peasant vegetable dishes (often including bread or potatoes) of the sort you can trot a mouse on: like *oliagua* soups and *tumbet*. The islands also make excellent large pies and pizza-like *cocas*.

Montserrat monastery, the national shrine of Catalonia, where
Wagner had his inspiration for "Parsifal."

CHAPTER I

Andalusia

◆

*Andalusia forms the whole of the south, stretching from
Huelva on the Atlantic to Almería deep into the
Mediterranean. It embraces two sunshine Spains – the
tourist beaches and the world of flamenco and bullfighting.
Here you can eat the food of the Moors – chilled soups,
skewered meats, and tiny almond sweetmeats – and also
that of the gypsies. It is the land of olives, oranges and the
refreshing iced red wine cup,* sangría.

14

Icy Red Gazpacho Soup

GAZPACHO ROJO

An icy, vinegared soup, made creamy with bread and oil, the basic recipe probably dates back to the Romans. Peppers and tomatoes were added after Columbus's voyage. In Arab times it was prepared by pounding everything in a big stone mortar, but now every farm owns a battery whisk to chop the vegetables in a big, wide-mouthed bowl. In Spanish restaurants it is garnished with lots of extras from little bowls.

SERVES 6

2 slices stale white bread, crusts removed	1 large red bell pepper, seeded and roughly chopped
1 small onion, chopped	4–5 big ripe red tomatoes, skinned and seeded
2 garlic cloves, finely chopped	3 tbsp red-wine or sherry vinegar
3 tbsp olive oil	3 cups iced water
1 tsp coarse salt	pinch cayenne
1 cucumber, seeded and chopped, with some skin removed	

TO GARNISH CHOOSE FROM

1/3 cup fried croûtons	1/3 cup chopped Spanish onion or green onions
2 hard-boiled eggs, peeled and chopped	green or black olives, pitted and chopped
1/3 cup chopped bell pepper (red, green or both)	

Soak the bread in water, then squeeze out. Put it in a blender or food processor with the onion, garlic, olive oil, and salt and purée.

Add the cucumber to the blender or food processor with the pepper, then the tomatoes and vinegar (you may have to do this in two batches in a small machine). Chill for at least 12 hours, preferably overnight, or freeze for about 30 minutes.

To serve, dilute with iced water (no ice cubes) and season to taste with the cayenne. Arrange the garnishes in little dishes and pass them around on a tray for everyone to help themselves.

Kidneys in Sherry

○

RIÑONES AL JEREZ

Most *tapas* bars in Spain serve this dish, though at home it can be served with rice or pasta as a main meal. You can add sliced mushrooms to increase the number of portions.

SERVES 6 AS A *TAPA*,
4 AS A SUPPER DISH

10 fresh lambs' kidneys	*3 tbsp flour*
1 big Spanish onion, chopped	*¹/₂ cup fino sherry*
¹/₃ cup olive oil	*or Montilla*
¹/₄ lb bacon, ham, or	*1 tbsp tomato paste*
pancetta from an	*2 sprigs fresh thyme*
Italian delicatessen, diced	*salt and freshly ground black*
1 garlic clove, finely chopped	*pepper*

Fry the onion in 3 tablespoons of oil over a low heat in a big skillet. When it starts to soften add the diced bacon, ham or *pancetta*, and garlic.

Remove the membranes and cut out the middle cores from the kidneys, then cut them into large dice. Remove and reserve the onion and bacon from the pan, and add 2–3 tablespoons more oil.

Put in the diced kidneys, a handful at a time, over the highest heat, and stir occasionally. When they are sealed, pull them to the sides of the skillet and add the next handful. When they are all sealed and colored, return the onions and bacon, sprinkle with flour and stir in. Add the *fino*, tomato paste and thyme and bring to simmering point. Season to taste.

Moorish Pickled Anchovies

———◦———

ESCABECHE DE BOQUERONES

This is an old, old way of preserving small fish which has survived into modern times because it is so delicious. The coast round Nerva is known for its shoals of fresh anchovies. In Malaga the fish are pressed together into a little fan, four tails together, for frying, but this is not essential to the recipe.

SERVES 8

2 lb fresh anchovies, or sardines or smelts, etc.	*small pinch saffron strands*
	1 tsp cumin seeds
⅓–⅔ cup olive oil	*1 tsp ground ginger*
about ½ cup flour	*1 good cup red-wine vinegar*
salt and freshly ground black pepper	*4 bay leaves*
6 garlic cloves, finely chopped	*1 lemon, thinly sliced*

Cut off the fish heads, pulling out their innards. Slit them down the belly, as far as the tail, and swish the insides under a tap. Then put each fish down on a board, black back upwards, and press a thumb firmly down on it. This opens it out like a book and makes it easy to rip out the backbone and tail.

Heat ⅓ cup of oil in a big skillet. Dust the fish with seasoned flour on a baking sheet and fry when you have a trayful (there will be about 4 of these). Put them in skin-side down and turn after 1–2 minutes. Remove them to paper to drain. Take the skillet off the heat between batches and add more oil as necessary.

Fry the garlic in the remaining oil, then move to a mortar or a small herb (or coffee) mill. Work to a paste with a pinch of salt, the saffron, cumin seeds, and ginger. Work in the vinegar.

Arrange the fish in an earthenware dish, skin-side up. This can be shallow if you are planning to serve them within 24 hours, but should be smaller and deeper if you want to keep them.

Mix 1 good cup of water into the spicy mixture and pour this over the fish. Add more vinegar and water to cover them completely if you are keeping them. Lay the bay leaves and very thinly sliced lemon over the top. Refrigerate for half a day before eating. They can be served from the dish. They should be eaten within a week.

The flavor of garlic underlies many of the dishes in southern Spain.

Lima Beans with Ham, Ronda Style

○

HABAS A LA RONDEÑA

So popular is this fresh bean dish all over Spain that it is sometimes called *española* instead. It is made with raw *serrano* ham – the sierras of Ronda are famous for their hams from the black-footed pig. Another virtue is that it is attractive made with frozen beans. In summer, when parsley is almost unobtainable in the south, the garnish may be diced red pepper or tomato.

Fry the onion in the oil in a flameproof casserole. As it starts to soften, add the ham or bacon, and garlic and fry until lightly browned. Stir in the beans (frozen beans need no water; fresh ones need about ½ cup. Cover, and simmer until tender, stirring occasionally. Fresh or frozen they take about 10 minutes.

Season the beans generously, stir in the chopped eggs and heat through. Stir in the parsley and serve.

SERVES 6

2 lb young, shelled (or frozen) lima beans

1½ cups chopped Spanish onion

⅓ cup olive oil

1 cup diced raw ham, smoked ham, or back bacon

1 garlic clove, finely chopped

salt and freshly ground black pepper

4 hard-boiled eggs, peeled and chopped

1 tbsp fresh parsley chopped

Farmyard Chicken with Olives

─────○─────

POLLO CON ACEITUNAS

This is a favorite dish because sherry and olives set off the flavor of chicken so well. It is good served hot from the casserole, but better still jellied. Cutting up the chicken first means it takes less time to cook and improves the quality of the sauce, because it reduces the amount of liquid. In Spain it is served with bread, but rice (hot or cold) could be used.

SERVES 4

2¾ lb corn-fed chicken, quartered with backbone removed and reserved
2 onions, chopped
3 tbsp olive oil
3 garlic cloves, chopped
salt and freshly ground black pepper
24 green olives
¾ cup fino sherry or Montilla
2 bay leaves

Fry the onions in the oil in a casserole, adding the garlic when they soften. Salt and pepper the chicken portions and pack these neatly into the pan, with the backbone, putting the olives in the spaces. Add the *fino* and bay leaves and pour in water to almost cover 1½ cups. Simmer, covered, for 30–35 minutes.

Spoon the chicken from the casserole, allow to cool for a few minutes, then remove the bones and skin. Return these to the liquid and boil for a further 10 minutes, to strengthen the jelly and increase its flavor. Check the seasonings.

Meanwhile split the cooked chicken into smaller pieces, arrange them in a shallow dish and distribute the olives. Strain the juices into a bowl and skim off all fat. Pour over the chicken and chill until the jelly has set.

Duck with Oranges and Olives, Seville Style

PATO A LA SEVILLANA

The original "duck with orange" comes from the city that introduced bitter oranges to Europe in the 11th century. Their juice and the olives make the duck seem fatless. Since it is a party dish, an elegant modern presentation is given here.

SERVES 4

1 oven-ready duck (preferably grey barbary)	1 Seville orange (or 1 sweet orange plus ½ lemon)
salt and freshly ground black pepper	1 bay leaf
3 tbsp olive oil	8–10 parsley stalks, bruised
1 onion, finely chopped	¾–1¼ cups duck broth from giblets (or chicken broth)
1 green bell pepper, seeded and chopped	2 large winter carrots
1 large tomato, skinned, seeded and chopped	1¼ cups green olives, rinsed
1 tbsp flour	
¾ cup fino sherry or Montilla	

Quarter the duck, removing the backbone, visible fat and hanging skin, Season and prick the remaining skin well. Heat the oil in a small casserole and brown the duck on all sides.

Remove the duck and all but 3 tablespoons of fat from the casserole. Fry the onion in this fat until soft, adding the pepper and tomato halfway through. Sprinkle with flour and stir in. Add the *fino* and stir until simmering.

Fit the duck pieces back into the casserole compactly, tucking in the backbone and 2 strips of thinly pared orange zest. Slice the orange (and lemon, if using) – do not peel it – and tuck these around the duck, pushing in the bay leaf and parsley stalks. Add enough broth to almost cover, and simmer, with the lid on, for 45 minutes.

Quarter the carrots lengthwise, remove the cores, and cut them into olive-sized lengths. Round the corners with a knife to make oval shapes. Simmer them in boiling water for 5 minutes.

Remove the duck pieces and discard the backbone, parsley stalks, orange strips and bay leaf. Purée the sauce through a vegetable mill (better than a blender). Return the duck to the casserole and pour in the sauce.

Add the olives and carrot shapes and simmer for another 10 minutes until the carrots are tender.

Move the duck pieces to a serving dish with a slotted spoon. Surround with the carrots and olives and keep warm. If there is too much sauce, boil to reduce it a little. Any floating fat can be removed by pulling strips of paper towels, across the surface. Check the seasonings, pour the sauce over the duck and serve.

Muscatel Ice Cream

HELADO DE PASAS DE MÁLAGA

Desserts here in the south come in a glass: super sweet *olorosos*, Málaga dessert wines – which are like sipping golden raisins – and wines made from the Pedro Ximénez grape, or sweetened with it, as are some of the cream sherries. Viña 25 is one to look for. Here is a dessert that can be eaten with a spoon. Ice cream (usually bought rather than home-made) is enormously popular in Spain but few are as good as this.

SERVES 4

⅔ cup muscatel raisins
vanilla ice cream to serve 4

1 good cup Málaga
wine or sweet oloroso
sherry

Pour about ⅓ cup of boiling water over the raisins and soak for 2 hours. Drain and fold them into the vanilla ice cream, then spoon into 4 bowls. Pour the wine or sherry over and serve.

Creamy Chilled Rice

○

ARROZ CON LECHE

This dessert is served in the deep south for spoiling invalids and children, and it was taken to Paris by Eugenia de Montijo, to become *riz à l'impératrice*. It is normally dusted with cinnamon, but can be decorated with mandarin segments or grapes.

SERVES 6

1/4 cup short-grain rice
5¾ cups milk
vanilla pod, split in 2
1 good cup superfine sugar
6 egg yolks

powdered cinnamon
2 lemons
1 cup double or whipping cream

Wash the rice in a strainer under running water. Tip it into a pan of boiling water and cook for 5 minutes, then drain well.

Heat good 2 cups of milk in a pan and add the rice, half the vanilla pod and ⅓ cup of sugar. Simmer until the rice has expanded and the mixture is thick (25 minutes or so). Cream the egg yolks with the remaining sugar in a heatproof bowl that fits over a pan of simmering water. Heat the remaining milk and pour it into the egg and sugar mixture, adding the rest of the vanilla pod. Cook gently, stirring, until the custard coats the back of a spoon. Remove the vanilla pod. Stir the rice into the custard with a pinch of cinnamon and leave until cold.

Cut 6 round discs of peel from the side of the lemons. Blanch them in boiling water for 2 minutes, then drain and refresh them under the cold tap. Whip the cream and fold into the rice. Turn into a shallow bowl and push the lemon peel into the rice at regular intervals. Chill well. Before serving, dust cinnamon over the top.

The Moors built many fountains and their designs have been much copied over the years.

CHAPTER 2

Extremadura

*P*igs and sheep outnumber people in these empty lands of the west. People have been leaving in search of a fortune ever since the conquistadores *left to discover Latin America. Famed for its hams and sausages, the rolling countryside has great beauty. The modest, generous local cuisine features the simple tomato and many wild foods.*

Granny's Garlic and Bread Soup

—O—

SOPA DE LA ABUELA

Bread and garlic soups are eaten for supper by the poor all over the country. This one is fortified with eggs and canned tuna, which I suspect has come to replace the traditional salt cod.

SERVES 4

6 garlic cloves
¾ cup olive oil
4 slices stale bread
1¾ pt light broth
4 oz can tuna, drained and flaked
salt

1 tsp hot paprika, or sweet paprika plus a pinch of cayenne
4 eggs
½ tsp cumin seeds, well crushed

Put the oil and garlic in a casserole over a medium heat. Remove and reserve the garlic the moment it looks cooked. Then fry the bread on both sides until golden. Add the broth and bring to a simmer, stirring to break up the bread. Add the garlic and flaked tuna and season with salt and paprika.

Break in the eggs and poach gently for 5 minutes. Sprinkle the cumin over the top before serving.

Fried Breadcrumbs with Ham and Peppers

MIGAS EXTREMEÑAS

Fried breadcrumbs are a popular supper or snack at any time of the day, usually served with a fried red *chorizo* sausage, or with fried eggs with paprika and a little vinegar dribbled over them. This version includes some extras and can be used to stuff a chicken for roasting. Good bread and plenty of fat will produce greaseless *migas*.

SERVES 4

4 thick slices stale country
   bread
salt and freshly ground black
   pepper
¼ cup bacon fat
¼–⅓ cup oil

2 garlic cloves, bruised
⅓ cup diced raw ham or
   bacon
1 small red bell pepper, seeded
   and diced

Remove the crusts and cube the bread. Sprinkle with water, season with salt and pepper, and wrap in a dish towel for at least an hour (traditionally overnight).

Heat the bacon fat and oil with the garlic cloves. When it smokes, discard the garlic and fry the ham or bacon, and pepper. When they are done, remove them and add the cubes of bread. Cook these for 12–15 minutes, moving them constantly. When crisp, return the ham and pepper and season to taste.

Baked Tomatoes with Ham and Egg

———○———

TOMATES ASADOS

A simple dish of baked tomatoes, using ham which is made in such great quantity locally. A bonus is that the insides of the tomatoes can be simmered to make an easy sauce. Add ¼ cup of *fino* sherry and serve over green beans. A ½ lb tomato will hold one egg, a ¾ lb tomato will hold two.

Slice off the tomato tops and keep to one side. Excavate the tomatoes, salt the insides, and turn them upside down for 10 minutes.

Then season the insides with pepper and thyme, stuff with chopped ham or diced bacon, and break an egg into each one. Cover with the tomato tops again (to stop the yolks going hard). Bake in an oiled dish in a preheated oven at 350°F for 20 minutes.

SERVES 4

4 beefsteak tomatoes
salt and freshly ground black
  pepper
pinch of thyme

good ½ cup chopped raw
  ham, or ⅓ cup diced, fried
  bacon
4–8 large eggs
oil for greasing

Fried Lamb with Paprika and Vinegar

EL FRITE

Yearling lamb is fried and seasoned with the local paprika, the most aromatic and tasty in Spain, or with *guindilla* (shown in the picture left) which is Spain's hot chili. With it goes the cloudy local *cañamero*, which looks like beer, but tastes like dry sherry. Either of these makes a good accompanying drink.

SERVES 4

1³/4 lb tender lean lamb shoulder, diced
1 slice stale bread
1/4 cup red-wine vinegar
1/4–1/3 cup olive oil
salt and freshly ground black pepper
6 garlic cloves

1 guindilla, or 1/2 dried chili, seeded and chopped, or a pinch of cayenne
6 cloves
1/3 cup chopped fresh parsley
1 tbsp paprika, preferably from Jarandilla

Sprinkle the bread with vinegar. Fry it in a casserole in 3 tablespoons of hot oil and reserve. Season the lamb with black pepper and salt. Put the casserole over your hottest burner and add the meat in handfuls, with 3 finely chopped garlic cloves and the *guindilla*, chili, or cayenne, turning it and keeping it moving with a wooden spoon. Add more lamb as each batch is sealed, with more oil as necessary.

Crush 3 garlic cloves in a mortar (or an electric herb or coffee mill). Add the cloves and parsley and pound or mill everything to a paste.

Sprinkle the lamb with paprika, stirring in the paste and 1 scant cup of water. Cook, covered, until the lamb is tender (about 30 minutes) and the liquid reduced to a few spoonfuls. Finally purée the reserved bread and stir in to thicken the sauce. Check the seasonings before serving.

A stone coat of arms set into a house wall.

Chicken with Tomatoes, Pepper and Cumin

─○─

POLLO A LO PADRE PERO

A simple, spicy summer lunch for the parish priest, as the recipe name suggests. I am told that it originally comes from Zarza de Alange.

SERVES 2

1 poussin, about 1¼ lb, or 2 corn-fed chicken legs	*4 large tomatoes, chopped*
salt and freshly ground black pepper	*1 green bell pepper, seeded and chopped*
3 tbsp olive oil	*2 bay leaves*
2 onions, chopped	*1 tsp cumin seeds*
	2 garlic cloves, finely chopped

Split the poussin, cutting the backbone free, and rub salt and pepper into the flesh. Heat the oil in a small casserole and color the chicken on the skin side while you prepare the vegetables.

Add the onions, tomatoes, and pepper as they are prepared, tucking in the backbone (if using a poussin), and bay leaf. Cover and cook over a low heat for 15–20 minutes.

Meanwhile, grind the cumin seeds in a mortar, working in the chopped garlic. Remove the backbone, stir the vegetables gently and stir in the cumin paste. Cook for another 3–4 minutes, to allow the flavors to blend. Serve the chicken skin-side upwards.

Liver in Red Wine Sauce

HIGADO EN SU JUGO

Extremadura is pig and lamb country and liver is eaten on slaughtering day, while the rest of the pig is cured.

SERVES 4

1½ lb pig's or lamb's liver, sliced	1 tbsp flour
⅓ cup red-wine vinegar	1 tsp paprika
salt and freshly ground black pepper	½ cup red wine
	½ cup meat broth
1 onion, finely chopped	1–2 apples, in cored, halved rings (optional)
3 tbsp rendered fat, lard, or olive oil	

Slice the liver into fingers. Put in an earthenware dish, add the vinegar, salt and pepper, and stir. Marinate for 2–3 hours.

Fry the onion in the fat or oil in a shallow casserole. Before it colors, sprinkle with the flour and paprika, stir in, and cook a moment. Drain the liver (saving the juice), add it to the pot and fry for a few minutes.

Add the wine, meat broth and marinade juices and stir in. Add the halved apple rings, if wished, and simmer for 3–4 minutes. Check the seasonings and serve.

CHAPTER 3

New Castile
and
La Mancha

*T*he southern half of the great high plateau that forms the
center of Spain, below Madrid, is icy in winter. In summer
the sun beats down from a molten sky on fields of
sunflowers and Spain's biggest and poorest vineyard.
Known for Don Quixote and his windmills, Castile also
grows the finest saffron in the world. The climate favors
strong raw tastes and dishes flavored with thyme
and cumin.

Mixed Salad from Madrid

———○———

ENSALADA SAN ISIDRO

This is the opening course of the meal eaten during the festival of Madrid's patron saint, joyously celebrated in mid-May. A first-course salad is the common Spanish pattern, and an *ensalada mixta* will contain canned tuna and egg. What the British think of as a "mixed salad" – lettuce, tomato, onion and olives – is called *ensalada verde* (green things), because tomatoes for salad are always firm. Ripe red tomatoes are kept for making sauces. This recipe for vinaigrette is really delicious.

SERVES 4—6

1 lettuce (Cos or Iceberg), washed, dried and chilled

7 oz can tuna, drained

rings cut from the center of 1 Spanish onion or 1 white onion, sliced

2 hard-boiled eggs, peeled and sliced

1/2 cup manzanilla *olives or other small green olives*

2–3 tomatoes (optional), sliced or cut into wedges

9 oz can white asparagus, drained (optional)

FOR THE VINAIGRETTE

1 garlic clove, finely chopped

1/4 tsp salt

1/4 cup sherry-vinegar

pinch of paprika

freshly ground black pepper

scant 1/2 cup olive oil

First make the vinaigrette. Mash the garlic on a board with a pinch of salt, working with the flat of a knife or in a mortar. In a bowl or the mortar with the garlic, stir in the vinegar, paprika and pepper, then the oil.

Spanish onions are mild. To eat white onions raw, the rings are best soaked in water for 10 minutes. Drain and blot dry.

Line the base of a shallow salad bowl or platter with lettuce. Flake the tuna over it, decorate with the onion rings, sliced cooked eggs, and olives. Add the slices or wedges of tomato, and/or canned asparagus, if using. Sprinkle with some of the vinaigrette.

Pickled Eggplant

○

BERENJENAS EN ESCABECHE

Almagro, in La Mancha, is famous for its spicy pickled eggplant, which is found in the *tascas* (bars) at all the Spanish fairs. This is a recipe for tiny eggplants (I bought 20 for this weight). They are prepared to an old Arab formula, with hot spicy peppers. When cut they are pink inside and seedy, like some exotic fruit. Double the recipe to fill three 1-lb jars.

SERVES 6—8

1 lb eggplants, as tiny as possible	1 bay leaf
salt and freshly ground black pepper	1 sprig oregano
	2 guindillas or 1 dried chili, seeded and chopped
1 onion, finely sliced	scant ¼ cup red-wine vinegar
3 garlic cloves, in slivers	1 lemon, sliced
⅔ cup olive oil	chopped fresh parsley, to garnish
1 tsp paprika	
2 tsp coriander seeds, crushed	

Prick the tiny eggplants all over with a knife point. Larger ones must be cut into fingers, each with some outside skin. Pack them tightly into a saucepan, add salt and pepper and push the onion and garlic into the gaps.

Add the oil, spices, herbs, *guindillas* or chili, and vinegar, with about the same amount of water as vinegar to cover. Lay lemon slices over the top. Bring to a simmer, cover with foil and a lid, and cook over the lowest heat for about 15 minutes until tender. Move to a dish or sterilized glass jars and re-cover with the lemon slices and liquid. Best kept in the fridge for 3 days before eating. Sprinkle with parsley to serve.

Meatballs with Saffron

○

ALBÓNDIGAS AL AZAFRÁN

Spaniards love meatballs and eat them on many occasions. In La Mancha it seems that saffron goes into every dish too. The meatballs can be served plain, or with a simple sauce made by chopping, reducing and seasoning tomatoes, or with a saffron sauce as for *Conejo al azafrán* (see page 44), but omit the cumin.

SERVES 4

1 lb ground pork or veal (or half and half)	pinch of dried thyme
	½ tsp salt
⅓ cup ham or bacon	pinch of cayenne
2 slices stale bread	pinch of powdered saffron
pinch of finely grated lemon zest	2 large eggs
	½ cup flour
1 tbsp lemon juice	½ cup olive oil

Crumble the bread by hand or in a food processor, and process (or chop) the ham or bacon. Mix together the bread, meat, lemon zest and juice, thyme, salt, and cayenne. Stir the saffron into the eggs in a cup. Combine with the breadcrumbs to make a rather wet mixture. Put spoonfuls of the mixture on a floured baking sheet and roll to coat the balls with flour.

Fry the meatballs in the hot oil, shaking the pan to and fro every now and then, so they roll over and color to a good gold on the outside and are cooked through. They take about 10 minutes.

Simmered Summer Vegetables with Eggs

—○—

PISTO MANCHEGO

Good hot with poached eggs, this mixture is also excellent cold, with the eggs scrambled in and a little extra virgin olive oil poured over. It is always worth making double the amount of *pisto*, if you have time, for it also makes an excellent sauce for meat.

SERVES 4

2 Spanish onions, thinly sliced	3 big zucchini, sliced (unpeeled)
1/3 cup cubed raw ham or bacon (optional)	salt and freshly ground black pepper
1/4–1/3 cup oil	pinch of ground nutmeg
3 garlic cloves, finely chopped	1/3 cup finely chopped parsley
3 green bell peppers, seeded and chopped	4–8 eggs
5 big, ripe tomatoes, skinned and seeded	

Fry the onions (and ham or bacon, if using) gently in the oil, adding the garlic towards the end. Add the peppers and fry for 5 minutes. Add the tomatoes and zucchini, and cook over low heat, stirring occasionally until the tomatoes reduce. Season well, adding nutmeg and parsley.

The eggs may be broken into 4 "nests" made in the mixture, and lightly poached, or they may be scrambled in. The *pisto* may also be baked in a dish with the eggs in nests, which takes about 10 minutes in a hot oven (375°F).

Spanish Potato Omelet

—○—

TORTILLA ESPAÑOLA

Virtually every *tapas* bar and menu in Spain offers this dish, although it belongs here, in the center of the country. It should be thick, firm and cake-like, quite unlike the French omelet.

SERVES 4

1 lb potatoes, diced	*salt and freshly ground black*
¹/2 cup olive oil	*pepper*
6 large eggs	

A pan about 9 in across is right for this dish (a bigger one makes the *tortilla* difficult to turn). Heat the oil well, add the potatoes and stir them. After a couple of minutes reduce the heat and let the potatoes cook through, turning frequently so they do not color.

Move them to a bowl with paper towels at the bottom. Drain the oil from the pan into a cup and wipe out the pan with paper towels. Strain about 3 tablespoons of the oil back into the pan and reheat.

Beat the eggs together and season them well. Remove the paper from beneath the potatoes in the bowl and add the eggs. Pour this mixture into the hot oil, spreading the potatoes evenly, and let the *tortilla* set for a minute at high heat. Turn down the heat to cook through. Use a spatula to work round the pan edge and shake the pan to and fro occasionally, to stop it sticking underneath.

When the top has ceased to be liquid, cover with a serving plate and invert the pan to turn out. Add 3 tablespoons of the oil from the cup to the pan, reheat it and return the *tortilla*, cooked side up, to the pan and cook for a further 2–3 minutes. Tortilla can be served hot or cold as a *tapa*, a main course or a sandwich filling.

Partridges in Wine with New Potatoes

○

PERDICES A LA TOLEDANA

Shooting partridges is a common sport in the hills behind Toledo, where this dish comes from, and they are trapped all over the country as they fly through on their twice-yearly migration. The birds are set off beautifully by the piquant wine sauce.

SERVES 6

3 fat partridges, wishbones removed	*1 strip lemon zest*
salt and freshly ground black pepper	*¾ cup dry white wine*
	⅓ cup sherry vinegar
¼ cup olive oil	*about scant 1 cup chicken broth*
1 big Spanish onion, chopped	*24 baby potatoes*
3 garlic cloves, finely chopped	*chopped fresh parsley*
3 bay leaves	

Choose a flameproof casserole into which the birds fit snugly, then salt and pepper them inside and out. Fry the birds in the oil, turning them over and propping them against the sides of the pan, until they are colored on all sides. Remove and keep warm.

Fry the onion in the same oil, adding the garlic when it softens. Bed the birds down into the onion. Add the bay leaves, lemon strip, wine, vinegar, and sufficient broth to cover the legs. Simmer, covered, over a low heat for about 15 minutes.

Meanwhile, simmer the potatoes in boiling salted water for 10 minutes. Move to the casserole, pushing them into the spaces between the birds (add more broth if absolutely necessary) and cook until they are done.

Remove the potatoes and the birds. Halve the partridges and arrange in a warm serving dish, then surround them with the potatoes. Keep warm. Discard the bay leaves and lemon strip and blend the remaining contents of the casserole. Reheat and check the seasonings (if extra broth was needed, boil to reduce a little). Pour a little over the birds and sprinkle with parsley. Pass the remaining sauce around in a jug.

Castile has many castles, built as armies advanced to eject the Moors.

Rabbit with Saffron and Aromatics

CONEJO AL AZAFRÁN

Rabbit with the taste of La Mancha – highly spiced with thyme and also with cumin, which was introduced by the Arabs nearly a millennium ago, when they came to plant saffron.

SERVES 4—5

2¹/₂ lb rabbit, in pieces	1 good cup white wine
2 large Spanish onions, chopped	15 black peppercorns, lightly crushed
²/₃ cup olive oil	¹/₄ tsp ground cumin
1 garlic clove, finely chopped	1 tsp paprika
30 saffron strands	pinch of cayenne
salt and freshly ground black pepper	6 sprigs of thyme
	1 bay leaf

Fry the onions slowly in 3 tablespoons of oil in a skillet, adding the garlic as they soften. Powder the saffron strands in your fingers and soak in ¹/₃ cup of hot water.

Remove the onion and garlic from the pan and add about ¹/₃ cup more oil. Season the rabbit and fry the meaty portions (back legs and saddles) for 10 minutes. Tuck in the thinner pieces and fry for about another 10 minutes until everything is golden. Remove the rabbit and drain off all the oil.

Add the wine and stir to deglaze the pan. Pack the rabbit pieces tightly into a smallish casserole and add the onion, wine, saffron liquid, crushed peppercorns, cumin, paprika, and cayenne. Tuck in the thyme and the crumbled bay leaf. Add ¹/₂ cup water to almost cover the meat. Cover and simmer very gently for about 1 hour until tender, making sure it does not get dry. Taste and add more seasonings – be as bold as you dare; you are unlikely to season it more than the locals do!

Sugared Toasts

○

TORRIJAS

Made with milk, these are a popular home-from-school treat for children. Made with wine, however, they are good enough for a dessert for adults. French bread looks more elegant than any other.

Heat the oil in a skillet and, when ready to fry, dip the bread rounds into milk or wine on each side and then into beaten egg. Fry on both sides, briefly, until crisp and golden. Drain on paper towels. Serve hot, sprinkled with sugar and cinnamon.

SERVES 3—4

*8 thick slices of stale French
   bread
about ¹/₂ scant cup milk or
   red wine*

*2 eggs, beaten
¹/₃ cup sunflower oil
sugar for sprinkling
pinch of powdered cinnamon*

CHAPTER 4

Old Castile

———— ◆ ————

The high heart of Spain contains the capital, Madrid, backed by the Sierra de Guadarrama, with the medieval cities of Segovia, Salamanca and Avila to the north. The struggle to eject the Moors left lines of castles across this country. It is now famous for its roast meats – tiny lambs and suckling pigs – but the common fare is beans, garbanzo beans, and lentils. This is also the country's bread basket while, in the river valleys to the north, some of Spain's best wine is made in Rioja and on the Duero.

Potatoes Made Special

—O—

PATATAS A LA IMPORTANCÍA

This is an excellent potato dish to precede roast meat, but it also makes a modest supper dish prepared the way I first had it, with a little canned salmon flaked over the top.

SERVES 4—6

4 large potatoes, diced
about ½ cup flour
salt and freshly ground black
  pepper
plenty of oil for frying
2 large eggs, beaten
1 onion, finely chopped
2 garlic cloves, finely chopped

½ cup dry white wine
pinch powdered saffron
1 good cup chicken broth
1 bay leaf
⅓ cup chopped fresh parsley

Turn the potato cubes in well-seasoned flour. Pour oil into a skillet to come one finger's width deep and heat. Flip the potatoes in beaten egg and fry in 2 batches, turning them and removing them to paper towels as they are browned and adding new ones to take their place.

Meanwhile fry the onion in 3 tablespoons of oil in a shallow casserole, adding the garlic as it softens. Add the potatoes, packing them in well. Pour in the wine, dissolve the saffron in the broth and add, together with the parsley. Season gently and simmer, covered, for 20 minutes. This very typical broth would suit other vegetables, for example courgettes, though this is not traditional.

Mild Cheese Custards

—○—

FLANES DE QUESO

Custards are part of Spanish culture – turned out from little tower molds – while caramel custard is the ubiquitous sweet. These savory custards make a soothing lunch, with tomato salad. They are flavored with a little chopped ham, mushrooms or cheese – whatever you have to hand. Cooked cheese, however, in Spain is unusual; cheese is normally eaten with bread. The famous local variety, Manchego, grates well and, like Parmesan, grows harder and stronger as it ages.

SERVES 4

4 large eggs	*¹/₂ cup grated Manchego, or*
3 tbsp butter	*3:1 Parmesan and*
about ¹/₄ cup stale	*Cheddar*
breadcrumbs	*salt*
1¹/₂–2 cups chopped	*ground white pepper*
mushrooms	
good 1 cup milk	

Heat the oven to 350°F. Grease 4 small castle molds (or a 3 cup ring mold) inside liberally with butter. Dust with the breadcrumbs to coat the insides, then tip out the excess. Stand the mold(s) in a small roasting pan.

Fry the chopped mushrooms in the remaining butter. Heat the milk to a simmer, then stir in the grated cheese. Beat the eggs, pour on the flavored milk, and season well. Pour into the mold(s). Distribute the mushrooms equally between them. Pour boiling water round the mold(s), to come two thirds of the way up the sides. Cook for 15 minutes for individual *flanes* or 20 minutes for a ring. Remove the mold(s) from the water and leave until cold before turning them out. Good with tomato salad.

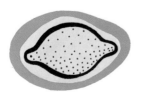

Orange Salad with Garlic and Red Wine

—○—

ENSALADA DE NARANJAS Y LIMÓN

A hot-weather salad, which also shows the strong connections of the west of Spain with the south. It is really a salad of left-overs, but can be very colorful.

SERVES 4

6 oranges	*1–2 garlic cloves, finely*
1 big juicy lemon	*chopped*
2 hard-boiled eggs, peeled	*salt*
3 ends of chorizo sausage	*1 cup red wine*
(or 1–2 thick salami	*¹/₃–¹/₂ cup olive oil*
slices)	*handful of green olives*

Peel and slice the oranges and lemon: 15 minutes chilling in freezer first helps to cut perfect, round slices. Then discard the pips, and put in a shallow dish.

Chop the egg white and *chorizo* or salami. Mash the garlic in a mortar (or on a board with the flat of the knife) and add a pinch of salt. Work in the hard egg yolk (in the mortar or a cup) and then the wine and oil. Pour over the salad. Scatter with egg white, sausage, and olives.

Uncle Luke's
Mildly Spiced Beans

JUDÍAS BLANCAS A LO TÍO LUCAS

A warming dish of spicy beans, made famous by a Madrid bar keeper in the 19th century. However, he actually invented the recipe in the south and the spicing is Arabic.

SERVES 6

1 lb dried haricot beans, soaked overnight	*1 bay leaf*
2 large onions, chopped	*2 tsp paprika*
3 tbsp olive oil	*1 tbsp vinegar*
scant 1 cup finely diced pork belly or ham	*¼ tsp ground cumin*
	pinch of ground cloves
1 garlic bulb, cloves peeled and finely chopped	*1 tbsp chopped fresh parsley*
	¼ tsp white pepper
3 tbsp tomato paste	*1 tsp salt*

Fry the onions gently in the olive oil in a casserole. Halfway through add the pork or ham, and the garlic. Drain the beans and add them to the pot with the remaining ingredients and water to cover them well.

Simmer for about 1¼ hours until the beans are soft, checking occasionally that they are not catching or drying out. There should be enough liquid left to give each person a couple of spoonfuls with the beans. Check the seasonings and serve in soup plates.

Perfect Plain Lentils

---○---

LENTEJAS A LA PERFECTA

In this part of the country, lentils are cooked with giblets or, in the same way as other pulses, with pieces of pig – ears, sausages, belly, and so on. Plain, they go well with fried fresh sausages, or *chorizo*, and I serve them with roast pork.

SERVES 4

½ lb green lentils	*1 slice country bread*
salt	*⅓ cup olive oil*
4 garlic cloves, finely chopped	*3 tbsp wine vinegar*

Bring the lentils to a simmer in a pan of water, adding salt only when they are done – after 30 minutes or so.

Meanwhile, fry the garlic and bread in the oil. When golden on both sides, put in a mortar or blender with the oil remaining in the pan, and purée. Add the vinegar. Pour off the water in the pan, except for a couple of spoonfuls, and stir in the paste. Simmer for a minute to let the flavors blend.

Fried Lamb with Lemon Juice

---○---

COCHIFRITO

The lamb of Old Castile is a wonder. In restaurants the animal is baked whole in great domed ovens. At home it is more likely to be fried simply with lemon juice. This is one of the nicest ways to cook fatless meat.

SERVES 4

1¾ lb trimmed tender lamb,	*2 garlic cloves, finely chopped*
in strips	*2 tsp paprika*
salt and freshly ground black	*1 good cup broth or water*
pepper	*juice of 1 lemon*
3 tbsp olive oil	*3 tbsp finely chopped parsley*
1 onion, chopped	

Season the lamb with salt and pepper. Heat the oil in a casserole over your hottest burner and add the meat in handfuls. Add the onion, too, and keep turning the meat around with a wooden spoon. Add more meat as each batch is sealed, with the garlic and more oil if necessary.

When the meat is golden and the onion is soft, sprinkle with paprika and add the broth or water. Continue cooking over a medium heat until the liquid has virtually gone.

Sprinkle with the lemon juice and parsley, cover, and simmer for 5 minutes. Check the seasonings before serving.

Quails in Knapsacks

─○─

CODORNICES EN ZURRÓN

The "knapsack" of the title refers both to the green peppers, into which the quail are stuffed, and to the hunter's bag. I suspect the recipe was devised for even smaller birds, attacking grapes in the Rioja vineyards! The Spanish love French fries, so oven chips are the ideal accompaniment for this dish.

SERVES 4

4 quails	3 garlic cloves, finely chopped
salt and freshly ground black pepper	2 tsp flour
3 tbsp olive oil	2 tomatoes, skinned
4 large green bell peppers	3 tbsp chopped fresh parsley
1 onion, finely chopped	½ cup dry white wine or good broth

Season the quails inside and out with salt and pepper. It is a good idea to remove the wishbone. Then brown them on all sides in the hot oil in a small casserole (one that has a lid).

Cut round the stems of the peppers and remove them, shaking out all the loose seeds. Then stuff the quails into the peppers.

Fry the onion in the casserole, adding the garlic as it softens. Sprinkle with flour and stir in. Lay the stuffed peppers in the casserole.

Add the chopped tomatoes, parsley, and wine or broth and season lightly. Cook in a preheated oven at 350°F for 40–45 minutes. Give everyone napkins, as there is a lot of picking up!

Boiled Meat Dinner from Madrid

COCIDO MADRILEÑO

Spain's national dish is based on a vast cauldron, which simmers away all day, hardly bubbling. In the old days households made it every day, for poached meat used to be the hallmark of the middle-class kitchen. From this pot comes a series of magnificent things.

First there is *caldo*. This is a clear broth, rich with many meat juices. Famous as clear soup with sherry in it, it is drunk world-wide. *Caldo* is also used in many, many Spanish dishes. It may be saved, but is often served as the first course before *cocido*, with a couple of spoonfuls of rice cooked in it.

The most important constituents of the pot are the meats, which are chosen for their diversity. Salt meat, fresh meat and sausage (preferably smoked) must all be there, for this is a dish for tough meats, full of flavor, which are made tender only by long cooking. A roasting chicken is less good than the cheaper boiling hen. Meat bones and trotters add richness to the broth.

The pot also contains vegetables, the first being garbanzo beans, which are the traditional, unifying element in all Spanish *ollas* (stewpots) and have an ancient history in Spain. With them come pot herbs – onion, garlic, and leek – each with their appointed time for being added and function. There are also fresh vegetables, to make colorful, cheerful platters to serve as an entrée to the meats, or as an accompaniment.

The order and manner of serving is governed by family tradition. Some families like a splendid display, with everything being served at the same time on different platters. This marks the occasion as a feast day, since the normal way is for vegetables to precede meat.

Often, and I think more conveniently, the vegetables are served first, garnished with the sausages. The practice has developed, now, of having a second pot for fresh vegetables – in the old days, I suspect, the life was cooked out of them. As the sausages are cooked with them, the second pot retains the cabbage flavors and the smoky sausage taste, which could otherwise reduce the value of the pure meat broth in the main pot.

When the meats, garnished with garbanzo beans, are served without fresh vegetables, a choice of pickles may be put on the table.

SERVES 8

1½ cups dried garbanzo beans, soaked overnight	1 whole garlic bulb
1–1 lb 10 oz uncooked, boneless corned beef in one piece	2 bay leaves
	8 black peppercorns, crushed
9 oz salt pork or fatty bacon in 1 piece, or fresh pork belly	1 small onion, studded with 2 cloves
1¼ lb ham knuckle with some meat attached	700 g (1½ lb) Savoy cabbage, quartered
	2 carrots, in big pieces
1¼–1½ lb beef marrow bone, sawn across	2 leeks, short lengths
	1 lb baby potatoes
½ a boiling chicken	2 chorizos, or other smoked sausage such as kabanos
1 pig's trotter, split	1 morcilla or 7 oz blood sausage

Several hours before cooking, cover the salted and cured meat (corned beef, salt pork or bacon, and ham knuckle) with cold water and leave to soak.

Choose a large stockpot – at least 1½ gallon. Pack in all the meat, skin-side down, with the beef bone. Fit the chicken and trotter on top. Add the garlic bulb, bay leaves, and peppercorns, and cover with water. Bring to a simmer, skimming off any scum that rises.

Drain the garbanzo beans, add to the pot, cover and simmer on the lowest possible heat for 1½ hours, checking occasionally. Halfway through add the onion stuck with the cloves. No other vegetables go in.

In a second large casserole, put the quartered cabbage, all the vegetables, and all the sausages. If the blood sausage has a plastic skin, this must be removed. Add water to cover the ingredients, and a little salt, and bring to a simmer. Cover and cook until the potatoes are ready.

Drain the vegetables and sausages and slice the sausages. Arrange the vegetables decoratively on a platter and put the sausage slices on top. This can be served before the meat or alongside it.

Remove the meats from the main pot, collecting the garbanzo beans together. Remove the marrow from the bone and slice it into the garbanzo beans. Slice all the meats. Arrange the meats and garbanzo beans on a platter, moistening them with a little broth.

Beef with Eggplant

——○——

R O P A   V I E J A

"Old clothes" is the literal translation of this dish, which sounds much more romantic than leftovers, although it means the same thing. Quick, colorful and satisfying, the overlapping slices look like much-patched jeans. Traditionally it is made with meat from the *cocido*. I make it from odd bits of cooked meat collected in the freezer and I like to include some garbanzo beans, as a reminder that they were in the original dish.

SERVES 4

scant 1 lb cooked beef or
    mixed meat (pork, ham,
    etc.), sliced
1 large eggplant, thinly sliced
2/3 cup olive oil
flour for dusting
1 onion, chopped
2 green bell peppers, seeded
    and sliced

1 garlic clove, finely chopped
14-oz can tomatoes
2/3 cup meat broth
pinch of ground cloves
salt and freshly ground black
    pepper
1/2 cup cooked or canned
    garbanzo beans

Slice the eggplant thinly, salt them and leave on the draining board for an hour. Blot with paper towels.

Heat the oil until it is very hot in a wide, shallow casserole. Lightly flour the eggplant slices and fry quickly in the hot oil, reserving them on paper towels. Remove all but 3 tablespoons of oil from the pan and add the onion and peppers.

When the onion has softened, add the garlic, tomatoes, and broth. Simmer for 3–4 minutes after adding the spices and seasoning.

Add the sliced meat, halve and add the eggplant slices, then the garbanzo beans. Simmer together for 3–4 minutes, after which time the dish should be pretty well solid. Check the seasonings.

The city walls of Avila. This stronghold was an important element in the defence against the Moors.

Drunken Cakes

—o—

BIZCOCHO BORRACHO

Guadalajara is famous for this sponge cake which, as the name says, soaks up a rich caramelized syrup and alcohol. I regret to say that Spain now squirts whipped cream over desserts, like many other countries, so if I make this for a birthday, I cut the sponge in two lengthwise and arrange them end-to-end on a long piece of marble. I pipe cream around the base (to stop alcohol dripping out) and again all round the top. It makes 16 slices, but half the quantity bakes satisfactorily in a low-sided fudge pan.

SERVES 12—16

6 large eggs, separated
butter for greasing
scant 1 cup superfine sugar
grated zest of 1 lemon

1³/4 cups flour
powdered cinnamon for
    dusting
whipped cream (optional)

FOR THE DRUNKARD'S SYRUP

1 good cup superfine sugar
1¹/4 cups boiling water

²/3 cup Málaga wine or
    Madeira

Heat the oven to 400°F and grease a shallow pan, about 12 × 7 in. Line the base and ends with baking paper, letting the ends hang clear, and grease again.

Separate the eggs. Beat the whites in a large bowl until they stand in soft peaks. With the same beater whisk the yolks in another bowl with the sugar and lemon zest until light and lemon-colored. Work in a little white into the yolks, to soften them, then fold this mixture into the whites with a hand whisk or big spoon. Alternately, sift flour over the top as you add the yolks and fold it in. Turn into the buttered pan, mounding it slightly in the corners, and bake for 15 minutes until risen and golden.

Let the cake set for 5 minutes, then turn onto a cake rack and remove the paper. Leave it to cool completely. Meanwhile make the drunkard's syrup. Put ¹/3 cup of sugar in a pan with 3 tablespoons of water. Cook until it caramelizes, shaking the pan a little to mix if one side browns too fast. When it smells good, dip the bottom of the pan into a sink containing cold water to stop it turning too dark. Pour in the boiling water and add the

rest of the sugar. Bring to a simmer, stirring until everything has dissolved.

Cut the cold cake into 12 squares and arrange on a dish, bottoms up. Add about three-quarters of the caramel syrup to the wine and feed the cake with alcoholic syrup. Turn the cakes topside up and pierce the baked crust with a skewer. Go on pouring syrup into the cakes (you will probably need the reserved syrup too). Dust lightly with cinnamon and chill for at least 2 hours. I think whipped cream goes well.

Galician Bean, Pork and Greens Soup

———○———

CALDO GALLEGO

Traditionally this is a spring soup in Galicia, made with the top spring leaves of turnips, *grelos*, and with *cachelos*, which are special seasonal baby potatoes. The flavor comes from salt meat: use fresh spare ribs or salt pork belly, whichever is easiest.

SERVES 6

1½ cups dried haricot beans, soaked overnight
¾ lb country-style pork spare ribs or 4 oz salt pork
salt
1 lb smoked ham knuckle bone with meat
1 lb baby potatoes
freshly ground black pepper
7 oz tender turnip leaves or kale

If using pork ribs, rub them well with salt. Alternatively, salt pork must be blanched. Put it with the ham bone in a pan, cover with cold water, and bring to a boil. Simmer for 5 minutes then drain. Cube the pork.

Drain the beans and put them, with the meat and bones, into a casserole. Add 4½ pt water, bring to a simmer, skim off any scum, then cook gently, covered, for 1 hour.

Add the potatoes and simmer until done (about 20 minutes). Remove all the bones from the pot and taste the broth. Season with salt and pepper as necessary. Add the greens and simmer for another 5–10 minutes. Return all the meat from the bones to the pan. To thicken the liquid a little, mash in a few potatoes.

St James's Baked Scallops

VIERAS DE SANTIAGO

Every restaurant in the old town of Santiago offers this dish on St James's Day, for scallops have always been identified with the Saint and scallop shells are still the badge of pilgrims to his shrine. Galician scallops are huge, with creamy orange roes and big white muscles. Tomatoes and brandy make a splendid sauce for them.

SERVES 4

14 oz shelled scallops (preferably 2–3 big ones on the shell per person)
1 tbsp butter
¼ cup oil
⅓ cup aguardiente (eau-de-vie) or brandy
1 onion, finely chopped
3 garlic cloves, finely chopped
7 oz ripe tomatoes, skinned and seeded (or use canned tomatoes)
1 tsp paprika
pinch of cayenne
½ cup dry white wine or fish broth
salt and freshly ground black pepper
about ¼ cup breadcrumbs
1 tbsp chopped fresh parsley

In Galicia the scallops are cooked in the curved upper shell. Ask for these at the fish market (or use small dishes). To clean fresh scallops, hold a knife flat against the shell and cut the flesh free, then remove the ring of gristle round the white. Pull away any dark gut at the root of the coral.

Heat the butter and 1 tablespoon of oil and quickly fry the scallops for 2 minutes on each side. Shelled or defrosted scallops make a lot of liquid, so remove them when cooked, then boil this off.

Warm the spirit in a ladle, flame it and pour over the scallops. Then spoon them into the upper shells or small heatproof dishes.

Add another 3 tablespoons of oil to the pan and fry the onion gently, adding the garlic as it softens. Add the chopped tomatoes, paprika and cayenne and cook until the tomato has reduced to a sauce. Moisten with the wine or fish broth, add salt and pepper to taste, and spoon over the scallops.

Mix the breadcrumbs and parsley and sprinkle thinly over the top of the scallops. Heat through for 2–3 minutes under a warm broiler and serve immediately.

Mussel Pancakes

—◦—

FILLOAS DE MEXILÓNS

Galician mussels are the best in the world and this simple recipe shows them off perfectly. The thin crêpes are related to the ones made in Brittany, which shares the same Celtic culture. Sweet ones are made with milk and filled with custard for dessert.

SERVES 6 AS A STARTER
4 AS SUPPER

4 lb mussels	*4 parsley stalks, bruised*
½ cup dry white wine	*6 black peppercorns, crushed*
3 tbsp chopped onion	

FOR THE CRÊPES

scant 1 cup flour	*⅓–½ cup thick cream*
2 large eggs	*about ⅓ cup butter*
mussel liquid (see method)	*½ cup chopped fresh parsley*

Wash the mussels, discarding any that are open (and do not close when touched). Pull off the beards. Put the wine, onion, parsley stalks, and peppercorns into a big pan and bring to a simmer. Put in the mussels (in 2 batches) and cover tightly. Cook over a high heat for 3–4 minutes shaking occasionally, until they are open. Discard the shells and any that remain shut or smell strongly. Strain the liquid into a measuring jug and leave to cool. Taste for seasoning.

Make the crêpe batter. Put the flour into a bowl or blender and work in the eggs, mussel liquor and 3 tablespoons of cream. (Don't overbeat in a blender.) Let it stand, if you can, for an hour.

Melt 1½ tablespoons of butter in a skillet, swirling it around. Add to the batter and stir thoroughly. Heat another ½ tablespoon of butter and swirl. Use about ⅓ of a cup of batter per crêpe: it is easiest to pour from a cup. Lift the skillet and pour the batter fast into the middle of the skillet and in a circle around, tilting the skillet to cover the base. (If you overdo the liquid, spoon off anything that doesn't set at once: crêpes should be thin.)

Put the skillet back over the heat, shaking it to make sure the crêpe does not stick. Cook for a minute until golden underneath, then flip over with a spatula (picking up with fingers is just as easy). Briefly fry the other side. Roll and keep warm on a plate while you make more.

Warm the remaining cream in a saucepan with the mussel bodies. Spoon mussels and a little cream onto one edge of a pancake, sprinkle with parsley, and roll up. Do not keep them waiting long.

Fresh shellfish are plentiful and delicious in Galicia.

Scrambled Eggs with Shrimp and Spring Leaves

REVUELTO DE GAMBAS Y GRELOS

Eggs appear on all Spanish menus, either as *tortilla*, in a firm cake, or as *revuelto*, which are stirred and soft. Shrimp are a popular addition too and this is an economical way to eat them. Turnip leaves are the favorite green accompaniment, but you could use spinach or kale. This is a lovely creamy spring dish, delicious served with crusty bread.

SERVES 4

9 oz young turnip leaves or spinach, washed, trimmed and torn into small pieces	8 large eggs
	3 tbsp milk
	salt and freshly ground black pepper
3 tbsp butter	
¾ cup shelled shrimp	3 tbsp oil

Blanch the young leaves in boiling water – just plunging them in and out – and drain well, then chop them. Heat the butter in 2 skillets until it is frothing. Divide the leaves between them. Add the shrimp and heat through (cook for 2 minutes if they are raw).

Beat the eggs with the milk and seasoning. Add the oil to the skillets, turn the heat to medium-high, and pour the eggs over everything, scrambling them lightly and stirring the outside to the middle with a wooden spoon. Divide the contents of each skillet between 2 plates.

Skate with Peas and Potatoes in Paprika Sauce

———o———

RAYA A LA GALLEGA

With a red sauce of oil and paprika, and green peas, this is the popular dish for every type of white fish. Try it also with monkfish. It is often garnished with strips of cooked red pepper, which enhance the coloring.

SERVES 4

4 portions of skate wing (or monkfish)	*9 oz shelled peas (or frozen peas)*
salt and freshly ground black pepper	*⅓ cup olive oil*
about 2 tsp paprika	*4 garlic cloves, sliced in rounds*
1 lb small potatoes, sliced	*1 tbsp white-wine vinegar*
4 small onions, sliced in rings	*2 canned pimientos or cooked red peppers (see page 78) – optional*
1 tbsp chopped oregano	
1 bay leaf	

Season the pieces of fish with salt, pepper, and paprika, and leave to marinate while you prepare the potatoes.

Meanwhile put the potatoes in the base of a wide flameproof casserole, cover with the onions, sprinkle with oregano, and add the bay leaf. Add water just to cover and put over high heat. Simmer for 15 minutes.

Fit in the peas and lay the fish pieces over the top. Turn down the heat, cover, and cook until the potatoes are done – about 15 minutes.

Drain off the liquid and measure good ½ cup of broth. Heat the oil in a small saucepan with the garlic rounds. When they start to color, remove the pan from the heat and add the fish broth, vinegar, and 1 teaspoon of paprika. Bring to simmering and pour over the casserole contents. Garnish, if you like, with strips of red pepper. Allow the casserole to stand, in a warm oven (or over very low heat), for about 5–10 minutes to let the flavors blend together.

Rabbit and Onion Pie

○

EMPANADA DE COELLO

Galician pies are large, double-crusted and flat, with ornamental edges. No festival is complete without a pie, but squares of cold pie go to work in lunch boxes too. Shellfish, pork with sausage, and game, such as pigeons (and thrushes in the old days), are common fillings. This recipe comes from Betanzos.

SERVES 8—12

1 rabbit, jointed
1 tbsp paprika
1/2 cup red wine

1/2–2/3 cup chopped fresh parsley

FOR THE MARINADE

salt and freshly ground black pepper
2 bay leaves, crumbled
4 sprigs fresh thyme
1 sprig rosemary

1 big Spanish onion, chopped
4 garlic cloves, finely chopped
1/2 cup red-wine vinegar
1/2 cup olive oil

FOR THE CORNMEAL PASTRY

2 3/4 cups all-purpose flour, plus extra for rolling
scant 1 cup yellow cornmeal
1/2 tsp salt
1 1/2 sticks (6 oz) cold butter or rendered fat, diced

2 small eggs
1 tbsp olive oil
1 tbsp water

Start a day ahead. Put the rabbit pieces in an earthenware dish, cover with the marinade ingredients and leave for several hours, turning if possible.

Turn again and put the dish in the oven preheated to 325°F. Let the rabbit color slowly for 1 hour. Sprinkle with paprika, pour the red wine over, and cook for another hour. Cool the rabbit and juices in the dish.

To make the pastry, mix the two flours and salt in a food processor. Work in the fat, then the eggs, adding 1 tablespoon each of oil and water, if needed, to make a rollable dough. Alternatively, work the fats and eggs into the flours with your fingertips, pulling together to make a dough. Chill for 20 minutes.

Prepare the filling by stripping the rabbit meat off the bones and shredding it. Rinse and trim the rabbit's liver, heart and kidneys (if you've got them), dice them, and then mix everything with the onion and dish juices. Sprinkle with some more red wine if the mixture does not look moist.

Preheat the oven to 200°C and grease a jelly roll pan – about 14 × 10 in. Divide the dough equally and roll out half on a floured surface, rather bigger than the jelly roll pan. Roll it up round the pin and unroll over the greased pan, leaving a border hanging over the edge. Trim the edges so they are just bigger than the pan, and keep the trimmings. Spread the rabbit over the pastry, leaving a margin round the edge. Season well and sprinkle generously with parsley.

Using the rest of the pastry, roll out the top the same size as the pan and lift the lid over, tucking it inside the pan's edge. Fold the outside border of pastry in over the lid, pressing it with a fork all along the edge, to bind the two together. Decorate the top in squares with long thin strips of pastry.

Brush the top with oil and prick with a fork. Bake in the oven for 20–30 minutes. Cool for a minute or so, then cut into squares. Eat with the fingers.

Mixed Fish and Shellfish Stew

CALDEIRADA DE PESCADOS Y MARISCOS

SERVES 6 OR MORE

2³/₄ lb white fish, cleaned

6 tbsp olive oil

1¹/₂ lb onions, chopped

1 lb clams, mussels etc., cleaned (see page 61)

salt and freshly ground black pepper

1¹/₂ tbsp paprika

10 black peppercorns, crushed

1 guindilla or ¹/₂ dried chili, seeded and chopped

freshly grated nutmeg

²/₃–³/₄ cup chopped parsley

³/₄ lb shrimp or small prawns

2 cups dry white wine

Cut off spines and fins from the fish with scissors and remove all scales by stroking the fish from the tail to the head with the back of a knife or your thumbs. Rinse the fish inside and cut off heads (freeze to use for stock). Cut whole fish across into sections 2 in long, and fillets into similar-sized pieces.

Warm 3 tablespoons of oil in the bottom of your chosen pot. Put in a good bed of onions. On this arrange a layer of one-third of the fish, choosing from the different varieties. Pack half the clams or mussels into all the spaces. Season with salt, ¹/₂ tablespoon of paprika, half the peppercorns, a little ground pepper, and *guindilla* or chili and the nutmeg. Sprinkle with 1 tablespoon of oil and plenty of parsley. Make a bed of shrimp or prawns on top.

Repeat all the layers. Make a top layer of fish, seasoning as before and packing onion into the gaps. Add more parsley. Add the wine and about 1 scant cup of water to almost cover. Then re-season the top layer, adding ¹/₂ tablespoon of paprika and another tablespoon of oil.

Bring to simmering (the best part of 10 minutes), then cover, turn down the heat, and simmer for 15 minutes. Check the broth seasoning and lay a spoon, as well as a knife and fork on the table, so that everyone can taste it. Take the shrimp heads off before eating, if you wish.

This recipe is a hymn to very fresh fish and straightforward to make because it needs no fish broth. This is a good dish for using a mix of strange fish that look interesting but you do not quite know how to cook! Do not include mackerel or any oily fish. Small crabs are welcome, though.

I buy half the weight in single fish like red mullet or small flounder (allowing extra for their heads), and half in fillets or steaks. For this small(ish) number of people you need a deep saucepan, 9 in in diameter (or perhaps a soup pot or deep pressure cooker), in order to assemble the layers of fish, which are part of the dish's charm.

Crisp Custard Squares

LECHE FRITA

The name means fried milk and the reason this dessert is so popular all along the north coast of Spain is that it combines a melting creamy center with a crunchy coating. Eat them hot or cold.

SERVES 6 OR 8

2¼ cups creamy milk
3 strips of lemon zest
½ cinnamon stick
scant ½ cup superfine sugar, plus extra for powdering
⅓ cup cornstarch
3 tbsp flour

3 large egg yolks
sunflower oil for frying
2 eggs, to coat
½–⅔ cup breadcrumbs (or dried crumbs)
powdered cinnamon

Bring the milk, the lemon zest, cinnamon stick and sugar to the boil in a saucepan, stirring gently. Cover and leave off the heat to infuse for 20 minutes.

Put the cornstarch and flour in a bowl and beat in the egg yolks with a wooden spoon. Start adding some of the milk until the batter is smooth. Strain in the rest of the hot milk, then pour back into the pan. Cook over a low heat, stirring continuously – it will not curdle, but it does thicken unevenly if you let it. Cook for a couple of minutes until it becomes a thick custard that separates from the side of the pan. Beat it hard with the spoon to keep it smooth. Pour into a small baking pan, smoothing to a square about 7–8 in and about ½ in deep. Cool and then chill.

Pour oil into a shallow skillet to a depth of about ½ in and heat until very hot. Cut the custard into 8 or 12 squares. Beat the eggs on a plate and lift half of the squares with a spatula into the egg. Coat and then lift them onto a tray of crumbs (big stale crumbs are best, but dried will do) and coat all round.

Lift the squares with a clean spatula into the oil and fry for a couple of minutes, shaking or spooning the oil over the top, until golden. Reserve on paper towels while you fry the second batch. Dust with sugar and cinnamon before serving. They can be served hot, but I think are even better well chilled.

CHAPTER 6

Asturias
and
Cantabria

---—◆—---

Asturias commands the center of the northern mountain range that parallels the northern coast. Facing the sea, the region is misty, green and apple growing, famous for its good cider and milk. This is also Spain's mining country celebrated for its flat bean dish, fabada. Cantabria is the corridor to, or from, the Basque country, a coast full of small bays and little fishing harbors, with the casino city of Santander.

68

Pink Santander Soup with Clams and Leeks

SOPA DE PESCADO SANTANDERINA

Spiny fish, like *cabracho*, that swim round rocks are the basis of this rather elegant soup. It is made for the summer visitors, who flock to seaside Santander.

SERVES 4

1 whole fish, about 14 oz (cabracho, snapper), cleaned	*3 tbsp olive oil*
	1 garlic clove, finely chopped
¾ lb firm white fish (monkfish, conger or cod)	*4 ripe tomatoes (skinned and seeded if using a blender), chopped*
2 onions, chopped separately	*2 leeks, washed*
1 bay leaf	*½ cup rice*
salt	*7 oz clams (chirlas)*
4¼ cups water	*ground black pepper*
⅔ cup dry white wine	*1 hard-boiled egg, chopped*

Simmer the fish with 1 onion, the bay leaf, a pinch of salt, the water, and half the wine for about 20 minutes. Strain, saving the broth. Remove the skin, bones, and head from the fish and flake the flesh.

Meanwhile, soften the second onion in the oil in a saucepan. Add the garlic, chopped tomatoes, and most of the leeks, chopped. Cook all this down to a sauce, stirring it occasionally. Then blend or press through a vegetable mill.

Put the purée in a casserole with the fish broth and the remaining wine. Bring to a simmer, add the rice, and cook until tender (about 20 minutes). Add the remaining leek, sliced into strips, and clams, about 5 minutes before the rice is cooked. When the clams open, give the casserole a good stir, and then add the fish pieces. Salt and pepper to taste and garnish with the egg on serving.

Fish Balls in Cider Sauce

———○———

ALBÓNDIGAS DE PESCADO EN SALSA

Ideal for people who cannot cope with fish bones, these fish balls are made from the belly and tail trimmings of hake (the favorite local fish), bonito, or perhaps soaked *bacalao* (salt cod).

SERVES 4—5

1³/4 lb very fresh white fish pieces, hake etc., skin and bones removed	2 slices stale bread soaked in ¹/3 cup milk
2 large onions, finely chopped (see recipe)	2 garlic cloves
	4 large eggs
about ¹/2 cup olive oil	salt and freshly ground black pepper
¹/2 cup chopped fresh parsley	¹/2–²/3 cup flour for coating

FOR THE CIDER SAUCE

3 tbsp chopped onion	4¹/4 cups fish broth
3 tbsp butter	strip of lemon zest plus juice of 1 lemon
3 tbsp flour	3 tbsp finely chopped parsley
1 good cup strong cider	

Chop the onions finely (in a food processor, if you have one). Fry in 3 tablespoons of hot oil until golden. Chop (or process) the parsley, bread, and garlic. Add the fish, and chop or process further. Add the onions, with 3 eggs, and season generously. Combine, making sure the mixture retains some texture. Chill while you make the sauce.

Soften the onion in the butter in a small saucepan. Stir in the flour and cook for 1 minute. Add the cider, fish broth, lemon zest, and juice, and leave to simmer gently.

Use a tablespoon to pick up the fish paste and roll into balls (golf ball size) on a floured surface. Beat the remaining egg on a saucer and roll each ball in it.

Fry the balls in olive oil until golden. Move to a warm shallow dish. Remove the lemon zest. Stir parsley into the sauce, season, and pour over the fish balls. Serve from the dish.

Fresh fish, including bream, pink grouper, cuttlefish, red mullet, and grey mullet.

Asturian Bean and Sausage Pot

——○——

FABADA ASTURIANA

The world's most famous bean pot comes from the wild mountains of Asturias. The beans are flavoured with local specialties like *lacón*, which is the cured front leg of a pig, and oak-smoked fresh sausages. Salt pork or cured beef make good substitutes. Cured sausages also go in, and give an incredible richness to the traditional white *fava* beans here replaced by lima beans.

SERVES 6

1 lb 10 oz dried lima beans	pinch of powdered saffron
1½ lb salt pork (or corned beef brisket or shank)	1 bay leaf
	3 tbsp oil (optional)
1½ lb smoked ham knuckle or hock, skin slashed	4 garlic cloves, chopped
	1 lb chorizos or smoked sausages, like kabanos
6 black peppercorns, crushed	
1 tsp paprika	6 oz morcilla or blood sausage

Choose a stockpot that holds at least 1¼ gallons. Cover the beans, in a bowl, with plenty of boiling water. Put the salt meat (pork belly, corned beef brisket or shank, and ham bone) into the pot and cover with cold water.

Bring to a boil, then drain the meat and return to the stockpot.

Drain the beans then add to the pot with the peppercorns, paprika, saffron, and bay leaf. Add 5 pts water. Bring slowly to a boil, then simmer very gently on minimum heat for 2 hours. A big pot on a small burner is best, and better still with a heat diffuser. Check occasionally that the beans are still covered, but do not stir (or they will break up).

Remove the ham bone and salt pork, to cool a little. Strip off the skin and fat, and take about 3 tablespoons of chopped fat for frying (or use oil). Sweat this in a skillet. In the fat it makes, fry the garlic lightly, then spoon it into the beans.

Fry the sliced sausages and *morcilla* or blood sausage (discarding artificial casings). Stir into the pot with the pan fat.

Remove all the meat from the ham bone. Chop it, and the salt pork or beef, and return to the casserole; simmer for a few minutes. Check the seasonings (there should be enough salt from the meat). This dish is distinctly spicy, so fresh green cabbage goes well.

Pot-Roast Chicken with Apples

POLLO CON MANZANAS

Chickens are all corn-fed on the north coast of Spain, where maize was first introduced in Europe. Delicious simply cooked with local apples.

SERVES 6

4¹/₂ lb corn-fed chicken	1 tbsp rendered fat or lard
salt and freshly ground black pepper	1 tbsp oil
1 strip of lemon zest	2 onions, finely chopped
1 garlic clove, bruised	scant 1 cup dry white wine or strong cider
3–4 parsley stalks, bruised	1 tbsp lemon juice
3 cloves	3 tbsp chopped fresh parsley
1¹/₂ lb dessert apples, peeled and quartered, cores and peel reserved	¹/₂ tsp powdered cinnamon
	2 tbsp whipping cream

Salt and pepper the chicken, inside and out, rubbing the seasoning well into the skin. Put the lemon zest, bruised garlic, parsley stalks, and cloves inside, with all the cores and apple peelings.

Heat the fat and oil in a casserole just bigger than the chicken. Put it in, one breast down, and turn it regularly, propping it on the sides so the legs become nicely colored. Finally set it back down, breast uppermost, and put the onions around it to soften.

Slice 1 apple into the onion, add the wine or cider, lemon juice, and parsley, cover tightly with foil under the lid, and put in a preheated oven at 350°F for 35 minutes.

Add the remaining apple quarters, sprinkling them with cinnamon, and give the casserole another 10–15 minutes cooking. Check that the chicken is cooked, then tip the juices inside into the casserole, and move the bird to a warm serving dish. Surround with the apples. Process the contents of the casserole, then return to the pot and heat through.

Check the seasonings, adding a little more lemon juice if needed. Stir in the cream and pass the sauce round in a jug.

Sliced Simmered Beef with Turnips and Carrots

○

ESTOFADO DE BUEY

It is very typical to pot-roast or simmer joints of beef in Spain, where the quality of meat is generally not very good. Roasting is a method reserved for very young animals. This is an excellent dish of sliced meat, served with its own root vegetables.

SERVES 6

3 lb beef rump roast, shoulder or shank, tied in one piece
salt and freshly ground black pepper
1–2 tbsp paprika
3 tbsp rendered fat or lard
3 onions, chopped
1 good cup cubed tocino, unsmoked bacon, salt or fresh pork belly
1 piece of bone, such as a bit of beef shin or ham knuckle

4 carrots, thickly sliced
4 small turnips, chopped in eight
2 sprigs of thyme
4 parsley stalks, bruised, plus 3 tbsp chopped parsley
1 sprig of mint
1 bay leaf
⅔ cup red wine
⅔ cup red-wine vinegar

Rub salt, pepper, and the paprika into the beef. Heat the fat in a deep casserole, which should be the right size to take everything neatly, and brown the meat on all sides. Then put the chopped onions round the meat and allow them to soften, adding the pork cubes and stirring occasionally.

Fit the bone, carrots, turnips, and the herbs (preferably tied round with a bit of string) into the casserole. Then add a little more seasoning and also the chopped parsley. Pour in the wine and vinegar and bring to simmering, uncovered. Fit a sheet of foil securely under the lid and simmer for 1½ hours very gently, until the meat is cooked.

Move to a serving plate and let the meat rest for 10 minutes before it is eaten.

Carve the meat in slices and arrange the vegetables and pork round them. Discard the bone and herbs. Blend the contents of the casserole and return to the pot to rewarm. Check the seasonings. Pour some gravy over the meat and pass the rest around in a sauce boat. Sprinkle with parsley.

Santander Chicken with Flavored Rice

POLLO CAMPURRIANO

A dish from farming country inland from Santander. Well-powdered with paprika, the chicken is fried, then cooked with ham and peppers, and served with rice. Small pearl onions can replace the green onions, but cook them in their skins for 5 minutes before peeling.

SERVES 4

4 small corn-fed chicken quarters
3/4 cup olive oil
salt and freshly ground black pepper
3 tsp paprika
2 tsp flour
scant 1 cup cubed streaky tocino or raw ham
1 red bell pepper, seeded and chopped
1 green bell pepper, seeded and chopped

8 fat whites of green onions or pearl onions (see above)
1 bay leaf
2 cups chicken broth
1 Spanish onion, chopped
2 garlic cloves, finely chopped
scant 1 cup paella or risotto rice, rinsed
1 good cup dry white wine

Heat 1/3 cup of oil in a skillet. Salt and pepper the chicken well, rubbing the flesh with 3 teaspoons of paprika, then dust with flour. Fry skin-side down over medium-high heat, for 5 minutes on each side, until golden. When you turn the chicken, add the *tocino* or chopped ham, peppers and the whites of the green onions.

Move to a casserole in which the chicken will fit tightly in one layer. Pack the chicken in neatly and sprinkle with the remaining flour. Tuck the green onion, ham, and peppers into any spaces with the bay leaf. Add just enough stock to just cover the ingredients – about 3/4–1 cup. Put on the lid and simmer gently.

Add the onion to the oil remaining in the skillet and fry until softened, adding a little more oil if needed. Add the chopped garlic cloves and the rice. Sprinkle with 1 teaspoon of paprika and stir gently. Pour in the wine and bring gently to a boil. Add 1 1/4 cups of broth and cook gently for 15 minutes. The broth should just be absorbed. Small quantities of rice can dry out, so watch for this; add another couple of spoonfuls of liquid from the chicken pot, if necessary.

When the rice is done, cover with foil and leave to stand off the heat for 5 minutes. Turn off the chicken too. Serve the two dishes together. You can sprinkle a little chopped green onion top over the chicken to garnish, if available.

Women washing clothes in one of the fast-flowing rivers typical of the region.

Schoolteacher's Hazelnut Macaroons

○

CARAJITOS DEL PROFESOR

Nut bushes and hens are part of the landscape here, so it is not surprising that nuts and eggs are used in the nicest cookies. Children eat these hazelnut macaroons with a glass of milk, for *merienda* at the end of the afternoon. They are named after a schoolteacher in Salas.

MAKES ABOUT 20

1¼ cups blanched hazelnuts
⅔ cup superfine sugar
finely grated zest of ½ a lemon

pinch of powdered cinnamon
2 large egg whites
butter for greasing

Toast the nuts in the oven while it heats to 375°F – for about 20 minutes. Grind them (in a food processor, do not over-grind them so that they start to turn oily).

Rub some sugar over the grater to pick up leftover lemon oil and then rub the zest well into all the sugar with your hands. Sprinkle with cinnamon.

Beat the egg whites until soft peaks form and then stir about a quarter of the white into the ground nuts to soften them. Sprinkle about half the sugar over the whites and gently fold in, then fold in the remainder alternately with the nut mixture.

Dot walnut-sized pieces onto greased foil on 1–2 baking sheets, pressing them out gently and spacing them 1 in apart. Bake for 15 minutes until golden brown. Let them cool for 5 minutes, then remove from the foil.

CHAPTER 7

The Basque Country

———◆———

A small province in the north, in the corner of the Bay of Biscay against the French border, the Basque country has an importance out of all proportion to its size – especially when it comes to eating! The food has a French polish and the region is home to Spain's very individual brand of nouvelle cuisine. The area is famous for fish, including salt cod and spider crabs, and sophisticated tapas, *while the locals have a taste for beans.*

Overcoated Shrimp

———○———

GAMBAS EN GABARDINAS

An extremely popular *tapa* in the Basque country, I believe the name, which means they are "wearing gaberdines" dates from the time that the Bonapartist army marched down from France in their waterproof capes. The lightest, crispest of batter coatings keeps the prawns moist in the hot oil.

SERVES 4

1 lb large shrimp, in the shell	*1 lemon, cut into*
olive oil for deep frying	*wedges*

FOR THE DEEP-FRYING BATTER

1 cup flour	*³/4 cup tepid water*
pinch of salt	*pinch of cayenne*
¹/4 cup oil or melted butter	*1 large egg white*

To make the batter, put the flour and salt in a blender (or bowl), work in the oil or butter, then the warm water to make a smooth batter. Add a little cayenne. Let this stand while you peel the shrimp.

Heat the deep-frying oil (to top heat on an electric fryer). Beat the egg white until it forms soft peaks and fold it into the batter.

Dip each shrimp into the batter and drop into the oil. Let them puff up and color for about 30 seconds, then remove with a slotted spoon on to paper towels. Serve at once with the lemon wedges.

Red Basque Pepper Omelet

PIPERRADA VASCA

This is an unusual egg dish for Spain. Both moist and soft, it shows the influence of the French Basque provinces which are only just over the border. The peppers are broiled and skinned first, until they are soft enough to melt into the eggs.

SERVES 4

1 lb peppers, red (or green)	1 lb ripe tomatoes, skinned
1 onion, chopped	and seeded
1/3 cup oil	6 large eggs
1 garlic clove, finely	salt and freshly ground black
chopped	pepper

Broil the peppers, giving them a quarter turn every 5 minutes, until they are charred on all sides. Put them in a plastic bag for 10 minutes. Then skin and halve the peppers on a plate, discarding stalks and seeds.

Meanwhile, soften the onion in 3 tablespoons of oil in a skillet until golden, then add the garlic and chopped tomato flesh. Chop the peppers well (or process them briefly). Add to the pan, with their juice, and cook to a soft sauce.

Beat the eggs, season and pour into the pan, stirring to make a soft, creamy, orange mixture, then fry like a French omelet, without stirring, until set underneath.

Salad with Roquefort Dressing

ENSALADA CON ROQUEFORT

I have at last worked out the magic attraction of Roquefort for the Basques: it touches the same taste nerve as *bacalao* (salt cod)! Roquefort dressings are fashionable in Madrid too and this one is first class.

SERVES 4—6

1–2 lettuces, preferably romaine, washed, cut across in hand widths and chilled

1 hard-boiled egg, peeled and chopped

¹/₃ cup shredded raw serrano ham (or substitute ¹/₃ cup diced fried Canadian bacon)

FOR THE ROQUEFORT DRESSING

3 tbsp crumbled Roquefort
3 tbsp thick cream
3 tbsp white wine vinegar
¹/₂–²/₃ cup virgin olive oil

freshly ground black pepper
pinch of hot paprika or cayenne

Arrange the lettuce in a wide, shallow salad bowl. Beat the first 3 dressing ingredients together then work in the oil, and season to taste with pepper and paprika or cayenne. Pour over the salad and decorate the top with egg, and the ham or Canadian bacon.

Potatoes with Cuttlefish, Clams and Peppers

PATATAS CON SEPIAS Y ALMEJAS

A simple dish of potatoes in a green sauce with sea flavors that come from two sorts of fish. A cuttlefish looks like a plump money purse with a frill around it and is best for stewing. They can be replaced by squid (a rocket with fins) but buy one big one, as little ones are too tender for anything but frying.

SERVES 4

2 cuttlefish (about 1 lb together) or squid
1/3 cup olive oil
2 garlic cloves
1 onion, chopped
2 oz diced raw ham or smoked bacon
1 lb clams or mussels, cleaned (see page 61), or 1 1/2 cups shelled cockles

2 green bell peppers, seeded and cut into strips
2 lb potatoes, peeled and diced
salt and freshly ground black pepper
1/2 cup chopped fresh parsley
5 saffron strands
1/4 cup white wine

Prepare the cuttlefish. Grip the tentacles and use them to pull out the insides. Cut across above the eyes and discard everything below. Large cuttlefish and squid have a mouthpiece in the center of the tentacles which can be popped out like a button.

Slit the body up both sides and remove the cuttle bone. Squid have a spinal structure like transparent plastic, which will pop out when the body is flexed. Rub off the skin with salt-coated fingers and wash. Cut off the squid's fins and cut the body into thick, wide rings. Rinse the insides and cut the rings into thick strips. Separate the tentacles.

Put 3 tablespoons of oil into a casserole and fry the garlic cloves until they color. Remove at once to a mortar.

Add 3 more tablespoons of oil and fry the onion and ham or bacon over a medium heat. When the onion starts to color, add the cuttlefish/squid and cook until the strips stiffen. Add the peppers and stir a couple of minutes. Pack in the potatoes and pour in 2½ cups of water to barely cover. Season with salt and bring to a simmer.

Mash the garlic in the mortar to a paste, working in 3 tablespoons of parsley, the saffron, and wine. Stir this, with some pepper, into the casserole. Cook until the potatoes are almost tender (about 20 minutes). Take off the lid halfway through, to evaporate some of the liquid.

Add the clams or mussels and simmer for 2 more minutes. Check the seasonings and sprinkle with the remaining parsley.

Belgian Endive and Ham Gratin

ENDIVIAS AL HORNO

This is one of the very few Spanish dishes to fit comfortably into international cuisine without an ethnic label. It was a fashionable supper dish in Britain in the 1960s.

SERVES 4

4 fat Belgian endive heads
salt

4 slices of raw or cooked ham

FOR THE BECHAMEL SAUCE

¼ cup butter
3 tbsp flour
1 good cup milk
½ cup grated Idiazábal, or a
* hard or Cheddar cheese*

freshly grated nutmeg
ground white pepper

Cook the Belgian endive heads in simmering salted water for 5–6 minutes. Drain, leave them a minute in the colander, then gently squeeze in paper towels to remove excess water. Wrap each one in a piece of ham and arrange in a buttered gratin dish just big enough for them.

Melt the rest of the butter, stirring in the flour, and cook a minute. Add the milk gradually, stirring until simmering, and then half the grated cheese. Season to taste with nutmeg, salt, and pepper.

Pour the sauce over the ham-wrapped Belgian endive, sprinkle the remaining cheese over the top, and brown under a hot broiler.

Salt Cod in Spicy Tomato, The Bay of Biscay Way

—◯—

BACALAO A LA VIZCAINA

A dish to show off the special flavor of salt cod. Like caviar, *bacalao* has an exquisite balance between salt and fish tastes – it is this that has gained it so many admirers.

The fish is sold in several different ways. The best and meatiest cuts are often sold separately and may be more lightly cured. You can tell what sort of salt cod it is by flexing the fish. If it seems slightly moist, it will hardly increase in weight on soaking and needs a maximum of 24 hours, but if the fish is stiff as a board and is a grey kite shape, it needs at least 24 hours soaking. It will then double its weight, but you will lose half that when the skin and bones are removed.

For this, the greatest Basque salt cod dish, I judge portions by eye, chopping out the prime pieces to soak and keeping the lesser bits for stews or salads (soaked *bacalao* can be frozen).

The scarlet sauce is flavored with a dried pepper that is spicy, sweet and mild. It is difficult to get outside Spain, but I find that tomato paste contributes a sweetness that can be balanced with cayenne.

*Many families in the Basque country make
their living through fishing.*

SERVES 4

4 portions of bacalao *(salt cod – see left), soaked overnight*
2 small red bell peppers
10 choricero *peppers (optional)*
1 bay leaf
4 parsley stalks, bruised
about 1½ tbsp flour
½ scant cup olive oil
¾ lb onions, sliced

3 garlic cloves
2 ripe beefsteak tomatoes, skinned and seeded
1 tbsp tomato paste (optional)
pinch of cayenne (optional)
1 tsp lemon juice (optional)
about ¼ cup stale breadcrumbs
about ¼ cup chopped fresh parsley

Broil the red peppers, giving them a quarter turn every 5 minutes, until they are charred on all sides. Put them in a plastic bag for 10 minutes. Then skin and halve the peppers, discarding stalk and seeds. Cut flesh into strips. Soak the *choricero* peppers, if using, for 30 minutes. Put the drained salt cod in a casserole with the bay leaf and parsley stalks. Cover with water, bring to the boil and remove immediately from the heat. Leave until cold.

Save some of the fish soaking liquid and remove any bones from the fish but keep the skin. Blot the fish dry, then dust with flour, and fry in ⅓ cup of very hot oil until golden (6–7 minutes). Reserve but do not try to keep the fish warm.

Fry the onions in the same oil. Before they color, add the garlic cloves and the chopped tomatoes. If you have *choriceros*, scrape the pulp from them and add it to the pan. Add 4–6 tablespoons of the reserved fish liquid. If not using *choriceros*, add the tomato paste and cayenne now.

When the sauce looks thick, purée it in a blender. Taste for seasoning: a little lemon juice will make it spicier. On the other hand if it is too spicy, ¼ teaspoon of clear honey will subdue it.

Pour half the tomato sauce into a gratin dish and arrange the pieces of fish on it. Cover with the rest of the sauce and decorate with strips of red pepper. Sprinkle with breadcrumbs and chopped parsley and heat through under a hot broiler.

Fish Stew with Red Peppers and Potatoes

———○———
MARMITAKO

A *marmitako* is the same type of earthenware or metal cooking pot as the French *marmite*. This dish is a stew made on board ship, so canned vegetables are commonly used, with an oily fish.

SERVES 4—5

1¼ lb bonito tuna belly or
   2–3 small mackerel,
   filleted
⅓ cup olive oil
1 onion, chopped
2 garlic cloves, finely chopped
salt and freshly ground black
   pepper
14 oz canned tomatoes with
   juice

3 canned pimientos
⅔ cup dry white wine
1 dried chili, seeded and
   chopped
1 lb potatoes, cubed
2 tsp paprika
3 tbsp chopped fresh parsley

Heat the oil in a shallow casserole big enough to take the fish. Fry the chopped onion gently, adding the garlic when it softens.

Cut the tuna or mackerel into serving pieces and season well. Push the onion to the sides of the casserole and fry the fish on both sides.

Add the tomatoes and *pimientos*, breaking them up with a spoon, and the wine and chili. Distribute the potatoes over the top, sprinkling with paprika and more salt and pepper. Add enough water to cover everything well. Cook for about 20 minutes or until the potatoes are done and the liquid has reduced somewhat. Check the seasonings, add parsley and serve in soup bowls.

Biscay Bay Sole with Cream and Shellfish

———○———
LENGUADA A LA VIZCAINA

The superb fish we know as Dover sole in the English Channel is fished all across the Bay of Biscay, right down to the Basque coast. This type of rich, old-fashioned cooking, with a cream sauce, has been typical for a century or more. Shellfish make the perfect garnish, and done this way they provide the broth for the dish.

SERVES 4

4 Dover sole (or plaice)
   fillets
3 tbsp chopped onion
6 black peppercorns
⅓ cup chopped fresh parsley
1 bay leaf
¾ cup dry white wine

16 medium-sized clams or
   mussels, cleaned (see
   page 61)
⅓ cup butter
about 2 tbsp flour
salt and ground white pepper
½ cup whipping cream

Put the chopped onion into a saucepan with the peppercorns, 3 tablespoons of parsley, the bay leaf and the wine. Bring to a simmer. Put in the clams or mussels, cover and cook for 1–2 minutes until they open. Remove the shellfish, then let the liquid boil for 5 minutes and reserve. Take one shell off each mussel (discarding any that are still shut).

Melt the butter in a skillet. Dust the fish fillets in 1 tablespoon seasoned flour and fry (probably 2 at a time) for a couple of minutes on each side. Remove to a warm serving plate and keep warm.

Add 1 teaspoon of flour to the skillet and stir into the butter. Strain in the reserved shellfish broth, add the cream and stir to deglaze the pan. Boil to reduce the sauce by half, adding the shellfish, face upwards, to warm them. This sauce should need no seasoning, but taste to check. Pour over the sole, sprinkle with parsley, and serve. Slim leeks make good partners for this dish.

T-bone Steaks with Cream and Armagnac Sauce

──○──

CHULETÓN DE BUEY A LA SARTEN, CON SALSA DE CREMA

Enormous steaks are typical of this part of the country where beef is aged, unlike the rest of Spain. Armagnac is local, coming from just over the nearby French border.

SERVES 2

2 T-bone steaks
3 tbsp butter
1 tbsp olive oil
25 black peppercorns

scant ¹/2 cup Armagnac or
    other brandy
salt
³/4 cup light cream

In a big, heavy pan, heat the butter, oil, and peppercorns. Add the steaks and cook over a medium heat until sealed on the outside, but still rare on the inside. Turn them over once more, pour the Armagnac or brandy over them and, standing well back, flame the pan, spooning the spirit over the meat until it burns out. Salt the steaks, move to warmed plates, and keep warm.

Add the cream to the pan and stir it with a wooden spoon until it reduces and thickens. Pour it, with the peppercorns, around the steaks.

Tolosa Red Bean Stew with Pork

◦

ALUBIAS DE TOLOSA

Tolosa is famous for its kidney beans which are long and as black as coal. Ninety years ago, however, they were red. Basques have always adored red beans and still do, so in this recipe they are red! The traditional dish contains the red *chorizo* sausage and the black *morcilla*, along with cured pork. It can work equally well as a starter.

SERVES 4

1 lb red beans, soaked overnight
5 oz salt pork or boiling bacon, in one piece
1 large onion, finely chopped
3 tbsp olive oil
3 tbsp chopped ham fat or more olive oil
2 chorizo sausages
1 morcillo or 150 g (5 oz) blood sausage, preferably made with onion
1 large green bell pepper, seeded and chopped
salt and freshly ground black pepper
2 garlic cloves, finely chopped

Drain the beans and put them in a pan with the salt pork and half the chopped onion. Add 1 tablespoon of oil and cover with at least two fingers' width of water. Bring to a good rolling boil then turn down the heat, cover, and simmer gently for 2 hours, or until the meat is almost tender. Watch that the water level remains high enough, adding more if necessary, but always in small quantities.

Fry the ham fat to give off grease or heat the oil in a pan. Slice and fry the *chorizos* and *morcilla* or blood sausage (removing any plastic skin) with the chopped pepper.

Remove the salt pork or bacon from the beans and chop it into cubes. Check the amount of liquid in the beans: it should now be well-reduced (if not then pour some off). Add all the meats to the pot and season everything well.

Fry the remaining onion in same pan you used for the sausage, adding the garlic at the end. Stir into the beans and simmer 10 minutes more.

Festive Walnut Cream

◦

INTXAURSALSA

A chilled walnut cream which is served as dessert on party occasions, like Christmas Eve.

SERVES 4

2¼ cups milk
good ½ cup sugar
strip of lemon zest
½ cinnamon stick
1 good cup walnuts
1 slice stale bread, crusts removed and lightly toasted
good ½ cup thin cream
powdered cinnamon

Bring the milk to a boil with the sugar, lemon zest, and cinnamon stick, and reduce the heat. Grind the walnuts in a food processor (be careful not to overgrind so that they start to turn oily). Add to the milk and simmer for 30 minutes. Crumb the bread and add it too. Simmer briefly then remove the zest and cinnamon. Beat with a wooden spoon (or process) to a creamy texture and stir in the cream.

Let it cook, then chill well, and serve very cold, lightly dusted with cinnamon.

CHAPTER 8

Navarre and Aragon

Together these provinces form a large part of the Pyrenees. Navarre is at an angle to the Basque country and to Rioja and has many of the virtues of both places. It makes fruity red wines, while the cuisine features splendid lamb. Down on the banks of the Ebro river grow a wealth of vegetables like asparagus, while wild mushrooms and game birds come from the mountains. Other Spaniards joke about the plain cooking in Aragon, a large and dusty province, but they have some fine dishes here and their sausages are truly excellent.

86

White Asparagus with Two Sauces

○

ESPÁRRAGOS CON DOS SALSAS

Great fleshy white asparagus is grown and canned in Navarre for the whole of Spain. You will need a jar, or two small cans for the recipe.

SERVES 4

14 oz canned asparagus or 16 spears, freshly cooked

FOR THE VINAIGRETTE

½ cup olive oil
¼ cup wine vinegar

salt and fresly ground black pepper

FOR RAW TOMATO SAUCE

1–2 ripe tomatoes, skinned and seeded
1 tbsp chopped Spanish onion

pinch of hot paprika or tiny pinch of cayenne
1 tbsp chopped fresh parsley

Drain the asparagus well and put it on a dish. For the vinaigrette, mix the oil, vinegar, and seasonings together in a jug. For the tomato sauce, chop the tomato flesh into neat dice. Mix in the onion and parsley and season lightly with salt and paprika or cayenne.

To serve, arrange the tomato sauce in neat piles round the asparagus and pass round the vinaigrette. Eat the asparagus with one sauce, then the other.

Mushroom-Stuffed Eggplants

BERENJENAS RELLENAS DE HONGROS

A simple but good starter before meat, or by itself a vegetarian supper dish, this is one of the few eggplant dishes that omits salting the flesh, and so is quick too.

SERVES 4 AS A STARTER,
2 AS A SUPPER DISH

2 eggplants, about ³⁄4 lb each	*salt and freshly ground black*
2 small onions, chopped	*pepper*
3 tbsp olive oil	*bechamel sauce (see page 81)*
3 garlic cloves, finely chopped	*¹⁄2 cup grated hard cheese*
2¹⁄2 cups cleaned and sliced	
mushrooms, preferably	
including wild ones	

Halve the eggplants lengthwise and remove the flesh carefully, so that the skin is not broken. Reserve the skins and chop the flesh finely.

Meanwhile fry the onions in the oil in a skillet until they color. Put in the garlic and mushrooms, and cook until they soften. Add the eggplant flesh and fry until golden, stirring occasionally. Season the eggplant skins and the flesh in the skillet, then stuff the skins with the fried mixture.

Pour a pool of bechamel sauce into a gratin dish. Arrange the stuffed vegetables on it, then dribble the remaining sauce into the eggplants. Sprinkle them with cheese, brown under a hot broiler for 5 minutes, and serve.

Well-Seasoned Mushrooms

HONGROS O CHAMPIÑONES AL VINO BLANCO

Wonderful wild mushrooms grow in the mountains, but this dish is good even with cultivated ones. Serve with fried or toasted bread.

SERVES 4—6

2 lb mushrooms (preferably including ceps), cleaned	2 garlic cloves, finely chopped
1 large onion, finely chopped	salt and freshly ground black pepper
1/3 cup olive oil	1/4 cup dry white wine
1 dried guindilla or 1/2 chili, seeded and chopped or cayenne to taste	3 tbsp brandy
	3 tbsp chopped parsley

Fry the onion in the oil in a large flameproof casserole, adding the garlic, and *guindilla* or chili or cayenne, once it has softened. Add the sliced mushrooms and fry until they soften. Season, and add the wine and brandy. Cook further to reduce the liquid a little, sprinkle with parsley, and serve.

Baked Salad of Red Peppers and Tomato

───○───

ASADILLA

The name of this recipe means "little baked vegetables" and this all-red salad is a summer favorite. It can be served with lightly toasted bread or decorated with anchovy strips.

SERVES 4

2 large red bell peppers	*1 tbsp chopped fresh*
2 beefsteak tomatoes	*marjoram*
¼ cup olive oil	*salt and freshly ground black*
2 garlic cloves, finely chopped	*pepper*

Skin the peppers. If you have gas, hold them on a carving fork in the flame, until black and blistered. Otherwise broil, giving them a quarter turn every 5 minutes. Put them in a plastic bag for 10 minutes. Then strip off the skins on a plate. Pull out the stems and discard the seeds, but keep the juice.

Meanwhile, skin the tomatoes, quarter them, and turn their seeds and juice into a jug. Slice the flesh lengthwise into strips and put into an oiled baking dish.

Slice the peppers the same way and mix in. Sprinkle with the garlic, herbs, remaining oil, and salt and pepper. Press the tomato and pepper juices through a strainer, add them, and mix everything gently. Bake in a preheated oven (at the highest temperature possible) for about 20 minutes, then leave until cold.

This is delicious as a salad, but it can also be puréed to make a sauce for chicken or fish. As it stores well in a screw-top jar in the fridge (for a week or more), it is worth doubling and trebling quantities.

Mixed Spring Vegetable Pot

MENESTRA DE VERDURAS

A dish which celebrates the new vegetables of spring – using a handful of this, a handful of that! Short lengths of leek, quartered baby fennel bulbs and the trimmed bases of artichokes (or whole baby ones) – whatever is available goes in.

SERVES 3–4

1 onion, chopped
3 tbsp olive oil
3 garlic cloves, finely chopped
1/4 lb streaky tocino or diced ham or bacon with some fat
2 cups shelled peas or lima beans (or frozen beans)
2 cups green beans, in short lengths

4 small carrots, thickly sliced
1/2 cup snow peas
1/2 cup dry white wine
1 1/4 cups chicken broth
salt and freshly ground black pepper
1/2 cup chopped parsley
1 hard-boiled egg, peeled, with yolk and white separate

Soften the onion in hot oil in a casserole, adding the garlic when the onion is soft. Reserve in a blender or food processor.

Fry the ham or bacon in the casserole in their own fat. Add the peas or lima beans, green beans, and carrots, laying the snow peas on top. Add the wine and broth, cover and cook until tender for about 10 minutes.

Purée the onion, garlic, egg yolk, and 3 tablespoons of parsley in the blender or food processor with a little of the cooking liquid. Stir this mixture back into the casserole and season well. Sprinkle with the remaining parsley and the chopped egg white.

Trout in Red Wine

—○—

TRUCHAS A LA NAVARRA

Trout crowd all the mountain rivers in Spain. There are two views as to what is the true Navarre way of cooking them. Some say they should be stuffed or garnished with fried ham or bacon – a method that is popular all over Spain. Other say they must be cooked with mountain herbs and the fruity red local wine, as in this recipe.

SERVES 4

2 small trout, cleaned	scant 1 cup Navarra red or another fruity wine
1 small onion, chopped	¼ cup olive oil
6 black peppercorns, crushed	salt
1 bay leaf, crumbled	½ tbsp butter
2 sprigs of thyme	½ tbsp flour
1 sprig of rosemary	¼ cup chopped parsley
4 parsley stalks, bruised	baby potatoes to serve
2 sprigs of mint, plus extra to garnish	

Rinse the cleaned trout, dry them, and pack them into a baking dish. Sprinkle with the onion, black peppercorns, crumbled bay leaf, thyme, rosemary, parsley, and mint. Pour in the red wine and leave to marinate for 2 hours or so.

Sprinkle the fish with the oil and a little salt and put the dish in the oven, at 375°F. Cook for 15 minutes for 9-oz trout, 20 minutes if they are any larger.

Drain off the cooking liquid into a saucepan. Mash together the butter and flour and drop it into the wine mixture to thicken it a little, stirring. Bring back to a simmer, then pour over the trout, and sprinkle with parsley. Serve with new potatoes cooked or garnished with fresh mint.

Spicy Lamb with Peppers

——o——

CHILINDRÓN DE CORDERO

Lamb from Navarre is famous and so is this dish. Old recipes use dried, pounded *choricero* peppers, but nowadays fresh peppers are used. It needs neither wine nor water to produce a succulent red purée that coats the meat perfectly.

SERVES 4–6

3 lb shoulder of lamb, cubed	*2 big baked red bell peppers,*
¼–⅓ cup olive oil	*skinned and seeded (see*
salt and freshly ground black	*page 78), or canned*
pepper	*pimientos*
2 onions, chopped	*3 tbsp finely chopped parsley*
2 garlic cloves, finely chopped	*1 bay leaf*
4–6 big ripe tomatoes,	*good pinch of cayenne*
skinned and seeded	

Heat ¼ cup of oil in a casserole, trim and season the lamb, and fry it in 2 batches, over a high heat until browned on all sides, then remove from the pot.

Fry the onions, with more oil if needed, adding the garlic at the end. Chop the tomato and peppers or *pimientos* finely (or process), then add them to the pot with the parsley, bay leaf, and cayenne pepper. Cook for a few minutes to make a sauce, then season and return the lamb.

Simmer for 1 hour, covered, over a very low heat. It makes its own liquid, but check occasionally that the heat is low enough so it does not dry. Taste for seasoning, paying particular attention to the balance of pepper and cayenne – the dish should be spicy. Surprisingly, you may even have to boil off excess liquid.

Chicken with Pounded Almond Sauce

——o——

POLLO EN PEPITORIA

The presence of this Arab dish is a reminder of their conquest here, right up to the Pyrenees. The sauce is thickened with spiced, crushed nuts.

SERVES 4

2¾ lb corn-fed chicken, in	*½ cup fino sherry or*
pieces	*Montilla*
2 garlic cloves, finely chopped	*1 bay leaf, crumbled*
about ¼–⅓ cup olive oil	*25 toasted almonds*
1 thick slice bread	*1 tbsp parsley, chopped*
salt and freshly ground black	*almost to a paste*
pepper	*pinch of ground ginger*
½ cup chicken broth	*pinch of ground clove*
10 strands of saffron soaked	*1 tsp lemon juice*
in a little broth	

Fry the garlic quickly in 3 tablespoons of oil in a wide shallow casserole. Remove to a blender or mortar. Over a high heat fry the bread quickly in the oil on both sides, then reserve.

Season the chicken pieces and fry them till golden on all sides (a corn-fed chicken should not need more oil). Remove from the pot and drain off any fat. Add the broth, saffron and *fino*, stirring to deglaze the bottom. Return the chicken pieces and add the bay leaf. Cook gently, covered, for 10 minutes.

Grind the toasted almonds in the blender or mortar with the garlic already there, adding the bread in pieces, the chopped parsley, and remaining spices. Stir this aromatic purée into the chicken juices, with the lemon juice, and serve.

Riverbank Hake with Young Green Vegetables

─────○─────

MERLUZA A LA RIBERENA

Along the banks of the Ebro, round Tudela, asparagus and other green things grow in the great vegetable garden of Spain. These wonderful vegetables set off the fish beautifully. Versions of this dish including shellfish are served in the Basque country as hake with *salsa verde* (with green sauce). But if it contains asparagus tips, then it comes from Navarre.

SERVES 4

4 pieces of hake fillet, about 6 oz each	*3 tbsp flour*
3 tbsp butter	*12 small asparagus tips*
3 tbsp olive oil	*¾ cup dry white wine*
1 onion, finely chopped	*1½ cups fish broth*
2 garlic cloves, finely chopped	*1½ cups peas, frozen or fresh, cooked*
salt and freshly ground black pepper	*½ cup chopped parsley*

Heat the butter and oil in a casserole into which all the fish will fit comfortably. Fry the onion, gently, adding the garlic when it softens. Season the fish and flour lightly. Push the onion to the sides of the pan and add the fish, skin-side up. Cook them slowly, turning them over once, until light golden, which will take 5–6 minutes.

Meanwhile cook the asparagus tips separately in boiling water for 2–5 minutes, depending on size.

Add the white wine and fish broth to the casserole and bring to a simmer. Add the peas and simmer for 5 minutes, then stir in the parsley and check the seasoning. Fit in the asparagus tips decoratively and serve in soup plates.

Braised Quails with Muscatel Grapes

─────○─────

CODORNICES BRASEADAS CON UVAS

Quails and grapes are seen together in the countryside and so are associated in the kitchen. Quails are often cooked wrapped in vine leaves. They are wild birds in Spain, trapped by nets as they fly through the mountain passes during migration twice a year. Look for plump ones when you buy them.

SERVES 3–6

6 plump quails	*4 black peppercorns*
6 strips fatty bacon	*2 garlic cloves, chopped*
¼ cup butter	*2 good cups muscatel or white grapes*
1 tbsp olive oil	*scant 1 cup dry white wine*
1 Spanish onion, chopped	*freshly grated nutmeg*
2 small carrots, sliced	*⅓ cup Spanish brandy*
2 tsp flour	
2 cups sliced button mushrooms	

Choose a flameproof casserole into which the quails fit with a small amount of room around them for vegetables. The pot size is important: if it is too big, more liquid will have to be used, and you will then have to boil to reduce it later.

Season the quails inside and out. Wrap them in bacon, starting from the back, around the legs to hold them, then parallel across the breast, stitching the bacon in place twice with a cocktail stick.

Heat the butter and oil in the casserole. Put in the quails over medium-high heat and cook, turning them on all sides, to crisp the bacon. Remove the birds from the pan.

Add the onion to the casserole and, when it starts to soften, add the carrots, sprinkling in the flour. Add the mushrooms and fry for 2–3 minutes. The easiest way to bed the quails in is to remove most of the vegetables, fit

in the birds, then stuff the spaces with vegetables. Put in a preheated oven at 375°F while you make grape sauce.

Crush the peppercorns and garlic in a mortar (or put them in a blender or food processor). Pip half the grapes and blend in, together with some of the wine. Pour this mixture round the quails, season with nutmeg, and add the rest of the wine and brandy.

Cover and cook gently for 30 minutes. Then add the rest of the grapes (they ought to be pipped, but not everyone does it), pushing them into the liquid. Warm through without the lid for 5 minutes and check the seasonings before serving.

CHAPTER 9
Catalonia

The eastern chunk of the Pyrenees, Catalonia, also includes the Costa Brava and Barcelona, which has a long history as one of Europe's best places to eat. The region is home to Spain's best white wines and Catalans challenge the Basques as inventive cooks. "Surf and turf," crème brûlée and allioli – copied throughout the Mediterranean – are but a few of their ideas, and there are also the superb fish and shellfish stews.

96

Catalan Mussel Soup

───○───

SOPA DE MUSCLOS A LA CATALANA

The best of the regional mussel soups, this has a hint of anis, though a big glass of dry white wine can replace the spirits. The initial part of the recipe also makes a good fish sauce or a *tortilla* filling.

SERVES 4

2 lb mussels	*salt and freshly ground black*
3 tbsp olive oil	*pepper*
1 mild Spanish onion,	*pinch of cayenne*
chopped	*juice of ½ lemon*
1 garlic clove, finely chopped	*3 tbsp chopped fresh parsley*
2 big, ripe tomatoes, skinned,	*4 slices of stale bread*
seeded and chopped	
½ cup anis, aguardiente	
(or Pernod)	

Clean the mussels. Cover them with cold water then scrub them one by one. Pull off all the "beards." Throw out any that are smashed or do not shut when touched.

Meanwhile, heat the oil in a casserole big enough to contain all the ingredients. Fry the onion gently, adding the garlic when it softens. Add the chopped tomato flesh and juice to the pan and cook until reduced to a sauce. Add ⅔ cup of water to the pan.

Add the mussels in 2–3 batches. Cook with the lid on for 3–4 minutes, until they open. Then use a slotted spoon to remove them to a plate and discard the top shell of each one. Throw away any that smell really strong or that remain obstinately shut. When they are all done, return them to the pan and sprinkle with the *aguardiente* or Pernod.

Add more water – about 1½ cups and bring back to simmering. Season with salt and pepper, adding cayenne, and lemon juice to taste and parsley. Break a slice of bread into the bottom of each bowl and ladle in the soup.

Potatoes in Spicy Tomato Sauce

───○───

PATATAS BRAVAS

The name implies that it is manly to eat these potatoes and, indeed, they can be so spicy that they are a challenge! They are ubiquitous in Barcelona's *tapas* bars and make a delicious starter at home.

SERVES 6 AS A *TAPA*,
4 AS A SUPPER DISH

1 lb potatoes, diced | *½ cup olive oil*

FOR SPICY TOMATO SAUCE

3 tbsp olive oil
1 Spanish onion, finely chopped
2 garlic cloves, finely chopped
3 ripe tomatoes, skinned, or 1¼ lb canned tomatoes

⅓ cup white wine or fino *sherry*
1 guindilla, ½ dried hot chili or a pinch of cayenne
2–3 tbsp lemon juice

Start with the sauce. Heat 3 tablespoons of oil in a casserole big enough to take the potatoes as well and cook the onion slowly, adding the garlic when it softens.

Meanwhile, fry the potatoes in a separate pan over a high heat in ½ cup of oil for 5 minutes, to seal on all sides. Then turn down the heat and cook for another 20 minutes, stirring frequently so they do not catch.

To continue the sauce, add the tomato flesh, strained juice or canned tomatoes, wine or *fino*, and *guindilla*, chili or cayenne to the first pot, and cook slowly until it thickens. Taste, add lemon juice, which strengthens the effect of the chili, and more cayenne if you like it hot. Add the potatoes to the sauce and cook until it is thick and coats the potato pieces. As a *tapa* they are served on a dish and picked up with cocktail sticks.

The porrón *from Catalonia has a distinctive shape and is unique to the region.*

Salad with Three Types of Cured Fish

———○———

XATÓ

Spain has a bigger range of cured fish than any other country around the Mediterranean. Here three of the common ones are combined in a green salad, with a sophisticated dressing of toasted hazelnuts and chilies. It is pronounced the way Americans say *château* – a good name for a dish with so much style. The cod should be free of bones and skin and soaked to the point where not all the salt has left it, so it is just poised between being salted and fresh.

SERVES 6

3½ oz soaked salt cod (see page 82)

1 chicory or escarole

2 oz can anchovies, drained

1 tbsp olive oil

1 tbsp sherry vinegar

⅓ cup romesco sauce (see page 101)

4-oz can tuna, drained and flaked

2 handfuls small green olives

Separate the chicory or escarole leaves, wash them, dry well, and put in the fridge to chill. Drain the cod and blot dry well on paper towels. Then pull the flesh apart with 2 forks into flakes and small strips that look like bits of wool. Cut the anchovy fillets diagonally.

Put the chicory into a big, shallow salad bowl. Stir the oil and sherry vinegar into the romesco sauce and check the seasonings – it should be distinctly piquant. Spoon this over the salad, and toss until it is well distributed.

Add the salt cod and the tuna, separated into its natural flakes, and toss again. Serve on individual plates, distributing the anchovy fillets and olives evenly over the leaves.

A selection of Spanish ingredients.

Spaghettini with Shellfish

———○———

FIDEOS CON MARISCOS

A simple dish in which a couple of types of shellfish, plus a few vegetables or herbs, flavor spaghettini. Catalans have been eating pasta for 500 years and the local versions is *fideos*, thin pasta in short lengths. Use whatever shellfish are available, like winkles, cockles and whelks.

SERVES 4

1 lb fresh shrimp in the shell
a fish head and bone
1 small fennel bulb with fronds
1 onion
5–6 parsley stalks
1 bay leaf
scant 1 cup dry vermouth or white wine
3 tbsp olive oil
2 garlic cloves, finely chopped
1 big ripe tomato, skinned and seeded

salt and freshly ground black pepper
1½ tsp paprika
8 saffron strands
2 cups clams or small mussels, cleaned (see page 61)
14 oz spaghettini
1 tsp anis or Pernod
lemon wedges
about ¼ cup chopped fresh parsley

100

Peel the shrimp and put the shells, fish head, and bones into a saucepan. Add the outer fennel and hard stalks, chopped, 3 slices of onion, the parsley stalks (snapping them up), bay leaf, and half the vermouth or wine. Add 4¼ cups of water and simmer for 30 minutes, then strain the broth.

Meanwhile, finely chop the remaining onion and soften it in the oil in a *paella* pan or shallow casserole. Add the garlic. Thinly slice the remaining fennel (reserving the fronds) and add about halfway through, while the onion is softening.

Add the chopped tomato and season with salt, pepper, and paprika. Powder the saffron with your fingers into a little of the broth.

Add the remaining wine, reserved fish broth and saffron liquid and bring to a boil. Add the clams or mussels and, when they open (discard any that do not), add the pasta and shrimp. Cook for about 10 minutes, stirring halfway through. The pasta should be well done and thickening the liquid slightly. Add the anis or Pernod, check the seasonings, and sprinkle with chopped parsley and fennel fronds. Serve with lemon wedges.

Flat Fish with Hazelnut and Chili Sauce

—○—

GALLO CON SALSA ROMESCO

Simply fried, flat fish are a treat when moist and slightly underdone. Small, whole fish cooked on the bone are best, but fillets may be easier. In contrast the sauce is famous and sophisticated.

SERVES 4

4 small lemon sole, about 7–9 oz each, cleaned, or 4 flounder fillets	salt and ground white pepper
	¼–⅓ cup butter
about ¼ cup flour	2–3 tbsp olive oil

FOR THE ROMESCO SAUCE

4 tbsp blanched almonds	½ dried chili or ½ jalapeño
4 tbsp blanched hazelnuts	chili, seeded and chopped,
2 garlic cloves, finely chopped	or a pinch of cayenne
⅓–½ cup olive oil	salt and freshly ground black
1 slice stale bread	pepper
1 big ripe tomato, skinned and seeded (or half a 14-oz can)	2 tsp red-wine vinegar
	⅓ cup fino sherry

Start the sauce by toasting the nuts in a low oven (320°F) for 20 minutes until biscuit-colored. Fry the garlic, then the bread slice, in ⅓ cup of oil and reserve. Add the chopped tomatoes and chili or cayenne to the pan and cook, stirring, until the mixture has thickened. Season with salt and black pepper.

Grind the nuts in a blender. Add the bread, garlic, vinegar, and *fino*, and pulverize everything. Stir this into the tomato sauce. Check the seasoning.

If you wish, the whole sauce can be blended once more to a pink "mayonnaise;" this makes a better salad dressing. Add a little extra oil for this second blending.

Strip the dark skin off sole, if you prefer. Dust with seasoned flour. Heat 3 tablespoons of butter and 1 tablespoon of oil in a skillet (if you want, use two skillets to have everything ready together, so repeat this). When very hot put in the fish. Whole fish need 3–4 minutes for the first side, 2 minutes for the second, fillets about 2 minutes each side. Serve on hot plates and pass the sauce around in a bowl.

Mixed Fish Stew with Garlic Sauce

○

SUQUET DE PESCADO CON ALLIOLI

A superb fish soup-stew from Empordà, with all the flavors of the Mediterranean. Shrimp, scampi and cuttlefish are often included for a party and this is an easy way to swell the recipe to increase the number of portions. If you can only buy cooked shrimp, lay a handful of these over the top of the cooking fish. A typically Catalan way of spiking up a sauce is to add a paste containing toasted nuts near the end. It is an easy way to introduce saffron, and is also a method of thickening the liquid. If any of the fish comes with its liver, this too is blended into the mixture. The dish is accompanied here by *allioli*, one of Europe's great sauces, and a creation that comes originally from the Catalan coast.

SERVES 6

2¼ lb edible fish: choose from firm fish (like monk, conger eel), flaky (like cod, gurnard) and whole (like red mullet, snapper, flounder)

3 tbsp olive oil

1 Spanish onion, finely chopped

2 garlic cloves, finely chopped

2 beefsteak tomatoes, skinned, seeded and chopped or 14-oz can

½ cup chopped fresh parsley

½ cup dry white wine

salt and freshly ground black pepper

1¾ lb baby potatoes

1 bay leaf

about 1 cup fish broth or water

1½ cups shrimp in the shell

FOR THE *PICADA*

pinch of saffron strands
1/2 cup toasted almonds
2 tsp sweet paprika

pinch of cayenne
1/4 cup dry white wine
3 tbsp stale breadcrumbs

FOR THE *ALLIOLI*

4 cloves garlic, finely chopped
1/2 tsp salt
2 tsp lemon juice

1 small egg yolk
3/4 cup olive oil, preferably
　Spanish

Heat the oil in a casserole big enough to take everything, and cook until the onion softens. Add the garlic, chopped tomatoes, and 1/4 cup of parsley. Add half the wine, season, and cook for 5 minutes. Then add the thinly-sliced potatoes, the bay leaf, and enough fish broth or water to cover them well. Season well and cook at an active simmer for 15 minutes until the potatoes are almost done.

Add the fish, cut into pieces of uniform size, plus the remaining wine: everything should be covered with liquid. Arrange cooked shrimp over the top. Put the lid on and simmer for 10 minutes.

Meanwhile, crush the *picada* ingredients to a paste in a mortar or an electric herb (or coffee) mill, starting with the saffron, almonds, paprika, and cayenne. Add this to the liquid in the pot as soon as it is ready, finishing up with the breadcrumbs and the remaining parsley.

To make *allioli*, crush the garlic with a pinch of salt in a mortar or on a board with the flat side of a table knife, scrape it together, and mash to a smooth paste.

Move the paste to a bowl and work in the egg yolk and lemon juice. In a bowl use an electric beater. Start adding the oil, drop by drop, until an emulsion forms and the sauce becomes rich, aromatic, unctious, and golden.

Put 3 tablespoons of *allioli* in a bowl, stir in a ladleful of fish broth, then pour it back into the casserole. People can help themselves to more sauce at table, if they wish.

Note: see advice on buying and preparing fish for stews, page 66.

A Catalan drinking from a porrón.

MAIN COURSE · SEGUNDO PLATO

Pork with Mussels

○

PORC AMB MUSCLOS

One of several dishes called *mar i muntanya*, sea and mountain, or, as Americans have it, "surf and turf." At first this was an economical way of eking out small quantities – almost like a starter and a main course put together to make one dish for 8 people! Later, simple mixtures like this one became more lavish, with combinations like chicken and lobster.

SERVES 8

1³⁄₄ lb lean pork, cubed
salt and freshly ground black
　pepper
3 tbsp rendered fat or lard
3 tbsp olive oil
1¹⁄₂ lb onions, chopped
6 garlic cloves, finely
　chopped
1-lb 12-oz can tomatoes
1 tbsp paprika

¹⁄₂ dried chili, seeded and
　chopped, or a pinch of
　cayenne
2 bay leaves
1 strip of dried orange peel or
　2 strips of fresh zest
3 lb mussels, cleaned (see
　page 61)
scant 1 cup dry white wine
¹⁄₂ cup chopped fresh parsley

Crème Brûlée Ice Cream

———○———

GELAT DE CREMA DE CATALANA

Custards are a basic part of Spanish cuisine in every region. The best of them, *crème brûlée*, may well have been invented in Catalonia. There it is served as a flat saucer of custard with the caramel lying in a net across it. This is done with a *quemadora*, a red-hot iron held over it, or under a big broiler in restaurants, but is more difficult to manage without them. The ice cream is easier, and popular too, for it is very rich.

SERVES 6

1¼ cups creamy milk (or 1:1 milk and light cream)	*4 egg yolks*
	1 tsp cornstarch
3 strips lemon zest	*⅓ cup granulated brown*
1 cinnamon stick	*sugar*
½ cup superfine sugar	*3 tbsp water*

Bring the milk to a simmer with the lemon zest, cinnamon stick and superfine sugar, stirring gently. Turn off the heat and leave to infuse for 20 minutes.

Beat the egg yolks and cornstarch with a wooden spoon in a bowl that fits over a pan of simmering water. Strain the hot milk into the egg mixture. Stir over simmering water until the custard coats the back of the spoon. Pour into a small bread pan, cool, and then freeze for 2 hours.

I have come to the conclusion that without special equipment it is easiest to make caramel in a small saucepan. Put in the granulated brown sugar and water, and heat until it smells well of caramel. Then, without hesitating, pour it onto a sheet of foil laid over a board. Wait until it has set and when it is hard, snap it up and grind (not too uniformly) in a blender or food processor.

Remove the custard ice cream from the freezer and beat well with a fork. Stir ¼ cup of caramel into the ice cream and freeze until firm. Soften in the fridge for 30 minutes and sprinkle with the remaining caramel before serving.

The Miro Gallery in Barcelona.

CHAPTER 10

Levante

Levante takes in most of the east coast: Valencia, Alicante, with its date palms and African climate, and Murcia, which remained under Arab rule until the 17th century. It also has many famous beaches. Valencia is known world-wide for its oranges and its rice fields. Paella was created here, barely 200 years ago, and there are scores more different rice dishes from this region. It is also known for fritters and turrón, a sweet, almond nougat.

Little Fried Pies with Tuna and Tomato

———◦———

EMPANADILLAS VALENCIANAS

These tasty little pasties are street food, sold at markets, and so are made with canned tuna.

SERVES 4—6

FOR EASY WINE PASTRY

3 tbsp sunflower oil	1/3 cup water
3 tbsp lard or butter	1 1/2 cups flour
3 tbsp fino sherry or Montilla	1/4 tsp salt

FOR THE FILLING

1/2 small onion, finely chopped	4-oz can tuna fish, drained, or diced ham
3 tbsp olive oil	1 hard-boiled egg, peeled and chopped
1 garlic clove, finely chopped	3 tbsp chopped fresh parsley
2 ripe tomatoes, skinned, seeded and chopped	oil for frying
zest of 1/2 lemon	parsley stalks
1 tbsp lemon juice	
pinch of hot paprika or a little cayenne	

To make the pastry, melt the fat or butter in the oil in a small pan. Remove from the heat and add the *fino* and water. Beat in the flour and salt, a little at a time, to make a smooth dough. Scoop from the pan and knead briefly. Put the dough in a plastic bag and chill for 2 hours.

Meanwhile make the filling – everything should be chopped to small, uniform dice. Soften the onion gently in the oil, adding the garlic halfway through cooking. Add the chopped tomatoes, lemon zest, and juice. Season with the paprika or cayenne and cook for 3–4 minutes. Stir in the flaked tuna, chopped egg, and parsley. Leave to cool.

Roll out the dough thinly on a floured surface and cut out 26–30 rounds with a large glass or 3-in pastry cutter. Put a heaped teaspoon of filling on each one, fold in half, pressing the edges together to seal. Keep them on a floured baking sheet.

Heat the oil for deep fat frying in a deep fat fryer (or deep saucepan) to its highest heat. Put in the pasties 5–6 at a time. When they bob up, spin them over with a slotted spoon and fry until they are an appetizing golden (2–3 minutes). Drain them on paper towels while you fry the next batch. Serve hot.

Finally, add some sprigs of parsley to the fat and this will take away the frying smells!

Deep-Fried Artichoke Puffs with Tomato Sauce

○

BUÑUELOS DE ALCACHOFAS CON SALSA DE TOMATE

Fritters are typical fare on the coast and are a legacy from Arab cuisine. They can be served with lemon wedges or with a tomato sauce made the traditional way with a *sofrito* base: onion softened in oil with garlic and parsley. These puffs are made with handsome globe artichokes, though 14 oz prepared bases could be substituted.

SERVES 4

8 medium globe artichokes
6 tbsp flour
salt and freshly ground black
  pepper

1 tsp baking powder
²/₃ cup beer
olive oil for deep frying

FOR THE TOMATO SAUCE

1 Spanish onion, chopped
3 tbsp olive oil
1 garlic clove, finely chopped
3 tbsp chopped parsley

2–3 big tomatoes, skinned,
  seeded and chopped
1 tsp grated lemon zest

To prepare the artichoke bases snap off the stalks (if these are stringy, the artichokes are tough and will need an extra 5 minutes' cooking later). Trim the bottom flat and cut through the top leaves just above the choke, leaving a base about 1¼ in deep. Trim away the side leaves with a small knife until the white bases show. Cook in boiling, salted water for 12 minutes, then drain upside down until cool enough to handle. Flip off any leaf stumps with your thumb, revealing the hairy choke. Remove it, leaving a smooth cup base.

Now start the tomato sauce. Soften the onion in the oil in a saucepan, then add the garlic and chopped tomato (and juice) with 3 tbsp parsley. Leave to simmer very slowly until the sauce thickens. To finish the sauce, check the seasonings and stir in the lemon zest.

Next make the batter by blending together the flour, baking powder, seasoning, and beer. Meanwhile, heat oil 1 in deep in a pan with sides. Halve the artichoke bases and dip in batter. Fry them in 2–3 batches, separating and turning them over in the oil with a slotted spoon. They will swell and bob to the surface and are ready when they have turned brown. Drain on paper towels and serve immediately with the sauce.

Baked Peppers with Rice and Meat Stuffing

BAJOQUES FARCIDES

The recipe name is the Valencian dialect name for rice-stuffed peppers – a recipe that has traveled round the world. This delicate version comes from Alcoy.

SERVES 6

6 big red bell peppers
about ¹/₃ cup olive oil
1 large chicken breast, diced
scant 1 cup diced lean pork
²/₃ cup diced ham or smoked
  bacon
scant 1 cup white rice
2 garlic cloves, finely
  chopped

2 lb ripe tomatoes, skinned
  and seeded, or 1-lb 4-oz
  can tomatoes
2 tsp paprika
pinch of saffron powder
salt and freshly ground black
  pepper
¹/₃ cup chopped fresh parsley
  and/or green onion tops

Heat the oil in a skillet and fry the seasoned chicken, pork and ham cubes or bacon until colored on all sides.

Take the pan off the heat then reserve.

Meanwhile, cook the rice (*paella* rice must be rinsed first) in boiling, salted water until done – about 15 minutes.

Add the garlic, chopped tomatoes (keep the skins if fresh), paprika, saffron, salt and pepper, and parsley and/or green onion tops to the pan containing the meat. Let the sauce simmer and reduce the volume of liquid by about half. Cut off "lids" at the stalk end and discard the seeds.

Oil a deep casserole (preferably earthenware), big enough to take all the peppers and make a bed in the bottom with the reserved tomato skins (if you have them). Check the rice seasoning, then ladle it into the peppers, and replace the lids. Cover the casserole with foil (originally a sheet of dampened brown paper) and put on the lid. Cook in the oven at 325°F for 1¼ hours.

Murcian Salad of Mixed Baked Vegetables

ENSALADA MURCIANA

An old method of making salad from cooked vegetables, they are baked round the barbecue in summer and then dressed to serve cold. The method is popular in Catalonia, too, where the dish is called *escalivada*. Here they are baked in the oven and make a good vegetarian main course. A variety of vegetables can be used – just adjust cooking times to suit them.

SERVES 8 AS A SALAD,
4 AS A MAIN COURSE

3 small aubergines (about 200 g (7 oz) each)
3 green peppers
4 medium onions, darkest skin removed
4 big tomatoes
1 bunch of spring garlic or fat spring onions, tips trimmed
8 tbsp olive oil
3 garlic cloves, bruised
juice of 1 lemon
salt and freshly ground black pepper
4 tbsp chopped fresh parsley

Preheat the oven to 400°F/200°C (Gas 6). Put the aubergines, peppers, onions, tomatoes, trimmed spring garlic or spring onions into 1–2 roasting tins with the oil and garlic cloves. A big pan will need 4–5 tablespoons of water to stop the juices burning.

Bake them for 25 minutes, then remove the tomatoes (you may also be able to combine pans at this point). After another 15 minutes, remove the peppers. Give the other vegetables a squeeze to see how close they are to being done. Put the peppers into a plastic bag as this helps with the skinning later.

The aubergines will probably be ready in about another 15 minutes, but onions usually need another 15 minutes or more. Stir the juices in the roasting tin and pour them into a cup, discarding the garlic cloves.

Skin the tomatoes whole and arrange them in the centre of a big platter, then just cut them across like a star. Skin the rest of the vegetables, slice them lengthways and keep all the juices they exude. Arrange the vegetables in sets on the platter radiating round the tomatoes. Arrange the aubergines so their exotic seeds are upward.

Sprinkle lemon juice over the salad and season. Then stir the reserved pan juices and dribble some into the centre of the tomatoes and over the salad. Sprinkle with parsley and serve.

Rice with Fish and Vegetables

————○————

ARRÒS AMB BONITAL

Easy, cheap and colourful, this rice and fish mixture is typical of Alicante. It is made with bonito (white tuna), though any firm white fish can be used. Artichoke bases are an alternative to the cauliflower or, in season, fresh peas. This is another recipe in which peppers partner saffron (the peppers are fried and pounded with the garlic). Here I have used a little extra paprika and tomato concentrate.

SERVES 6

500–550 g (18–20 oz)
  prepared bonito or
  monkfish
1 fish head for stock, rinsed
salt and freshly ground black
  pepper
5 tbsp olive oil
2 garlic cloves
1 green pepper, seeded
1 red pepper, seeded
150 g (5 oz) cauliflower in
  tiny florets

1 bunch green spring garlic
  bulbs or fat spring onions,
  chopped
1 big ripe tomato, skinned,
  seeded and chopped
1 tsp tomato concentrate
pinch of saffron strands
2 tsp paprika
tiny pinch of cayenne pepper
300 g (10 oz) paella or
  risotto rice, rinsed in a
  sieve under the tap

Simmer the rinsed fish head in 1 l (1¾ pt) salted water for 10 minutes to make stock. Meanwhile heat the oil in a 30-cm (12-in) *paella* or deep pizza pan and fry the whole garlic cloves for 15 seconds, then reserve in a mortar.

In the same oil fry the fish strips, seasoned with salt and pepper, and then reserve them. Slice the peppers and add, with the cauliflower and garlic or spring onion bulbs. Fry for a couple of minutes then add the chopped tomato and cook for another couple of minutes. Add half the fish stock and all the tomato concentrate and simmer the vegetables for 5 minutes.

Meanwhile crush the garlic to a paste with saffron and add with the paprika and cayenne pepper. Add the aromatic paste, the rice and the remaining stock to the pan and simmer for 10 minutes.

Stir the rice then fit in the fish pieces round the pan. Cook for another 8–10 minutes until the rice is done. Check the rice seasoning and sprinkle with a little chopped green spring onion top if you wish.

Saffron Rice with Chicken and Seafood

○

PAELLA VALENCIANA

This great star turn of the Valencian coast has always been cooked outdoors. Preparing it takes all morning and it is cooked by the men, so the whole thing becomes a party. The ingredients for it are rather special. It originally included snails and still has three sorts of beans in Valencia. This is a more modest version, but it still needs good broth and a suitably shallow, wide 13–14-in *paella* pan.

It speeds things up to prepare the base for the rice in the *paella* pan, and to use a second pan for frying the shellfish and chicken pieces.

SERVES 6

1½ cups paella *or* risotto rice	*pinch of cayenne*
about 6 tbsp olive oil	*6 chicken thighs or 3 legs, halved*
1 onion, chopped	
2 garlic cloves, finely chopped	*2 cups cleaned mussels (see page 61)*
5 cups fish broth	
scant 1 cup dry white wine	*1 tsp paprika*
40 saffron strands or large pinch saffron powder	*1 cup cooked green beans or peas*
1 cup raw shelled shrimp	*7 oz canned red pimientos, drained*
salt and freshly ground black pepper	*¼ cup chopped fresh parsley*

Fry the onion in 3 tablespoons of oil in the *paella* pan (the rice pan), adding the garlic when it softens. Warm the broth and wine together, soaking the saffron in a cupful of it.

Meanwhile, start a second skillet, heating 3 tablespoons of oil. Fry the shelled shrimp for 2 minutes (skip this if they are already boiled), then reserve. Rub salt, pepper, and the cayenne into the chicken pieces and fry for about 10 minutes on each side, adding more oil if needed.

Wash the rice in a strainer and drain. Add the rice to the onion in the *paella* pan, stir for a couple of minutes and sprinkle with the paprika. Add the saffron liquid and one-third of the broth and bring back to a boil. Set the kitchen timer for 20–25 minutes. When the liquid has been absorbed, add another third of the broth and distribute the mussels, shrimp, and beans or peas round the pan.

When the liquid has nearly gone, add the remaining broth and give the mixture its last stir. Add the chicken pieces, bedding them into the liquid round the pan. Simmer on the lowest heat (best on a heat diffuser) for about 8–10 minutes. The liquid should all disappear by the time the timer rings. Check that the rice is cooked.

Cut the *pimientos* into strips and lay these across the rice. Then turn off the heat and wrap the *paella* pan in newspaper or foil, to keep in the steam. Let is stand for 10 minutes. The flavors will blend and the last drop of liquid should disappear. Sprinkle with parsley and serve. Spaniards drink red wine with *paella*.

Pork Chops with Capers and Peppers

———o———

CHULETAS DE CERDO CON ALCAPARRAS Y PIMIENTO

Pork chops are Spain's commonest fare, cooked on *la plancha,* a hot iron, or fried. This colourful pepper and caper mixture has just the right acidity to balance the bland meat.

SERVES 4

4 pork chops	*1 red pepper, seeded and*
2 tbsp olive oil	*chopped*
1 small onion, chopped	*1 tsp paprika*
1 garlic clove, finely chopped	*salt and freshly ground black*
1 green pepper, seeded and	*pepper*
chopped	*2 tbsp pickled capers*

Heat the oil in a big frying pan and cook the onion gently for 10 minutes. Add the garlic and chopped peppers and fry, stirring occasionally, until the onions are soft (about another 10 minutes).

Sprinkle the chops with paprika – standard practice in Spain where paprika is the country's most important pepper and is used more than black pepper. Season with salt and pepper. Fry them in the pan, pushing the vegetables to the sides or piling them on top of the chops, until the chops are cooked and browned on both sides. Chop the capers roughly, stir into the peppers and heat through.

Rice with Pork and Spinach

───○───

ARROZ CON MAGRO DE CERDO Y ESPINACAS

"Sloppy" rice, *caldoso,* is the Spanish name for this type of dish, which is much easier to make than *paella.*

SERVES 4–6

350–500 g (¾–1 lb) lean pork, cubed
4 tbsp olive oil
salt and freshly ground black pepper
250 g (9 oz) fresh spinach, washed, trimmed and chopped

8 young garlic or fat spring onion bulbs
4 tomatoes, chopped
2 tsp paprika
350 g (12 oz) paella or risotto rice
pinch of saffron strands
1.25 l (2⅛ pt) light stock or water, warmed

Heat the oil in a *paella* pan or wide shallow casserole and fry the seasoned pork cubes. When they are golden, spread the chopped spinach over the top and cover with another *paella* pan, lid or baking sheet.

When the spinach has thoroughly wilted, add the garlic or spring onion bulbs and the chopped tomatoes, sprinkling them with the paprika. Cook gently until the tomatoes have reduced. Meanwhile, rinse the rice in a sieve, drain and add it with some salt to the pan and stir.

Powder the saffron into the warm stock with your fingers and bring to a gentle simmer. Cook over low heat for 15–18 minutes, until the rice is done. Check the seasoning and stir.

Iced Lemonade-Sorbet

───○───

GRANIZADO

Sitting out under the trees at night, waiting for the first breath of cooler air after a long, hot day, nothing is as refreshing as a lemon or coffee *granizado.*

SERVES 10

5 juicy lemons
500 ml (18 fl oz) boiling water
175 g (6 oz) sugar

500 ml (18 fl oz) cold water
10 glasses of ice slush

Wash the lemons and pare the zest from them with a potato peeler. Halve them, squeeze out the juice and reserve it. Put the zest in a bowl and pour the boiling water over it. Leave until cold.

Remove the zest and stir in the sugar and lemon juice. Leave to stand and stir again after 5 minutes, checking the sugar has dissolved. Keep it in a bottle in the fridge.

To serve, pour the lemonade into a jug and add an equal amount of water. Fill tall glasses with ice slush, pour the liquid over up it and drink through straws.

CHAPTER II

The Balearic Islands

*M*allorca and Menorca are Spain's biggest
Mediterranean islands, while Ibiza was the first hippy
colony in Europe. Many cultures have washed across these
islands, which grow capers, olives and almonds.
Ensaimada, *a snail-shape made in the lightest puff
pastry, and a smooth red sausage called* sobrasada, *come
from here. Mayonnaise was invented at Mahón in
Menorca, but in general the fare consists of rather solid
vegetable dishes and thick soups you could trot a mouse on.*

Fresh Shrimp with Caper Mayonnaise

GAMBAS CON MAHONESA Y ALCAPARRAS

Mayonnaise and fresh shrimp make perfect partners. Ironically, though, the bigger the shrimp are, the greater the weight you need to buy.

Mayonnaise was invented in Menorca and takes its name from Mahón although the French often claim the credit for having thought of it. I give the classic recipe and also the easier blender version which needs a whole egg. Contrary to general expectation, mayonnaise is not good made entirely with extra virgin oil – though it should have a faint taste of olives.

SERVES 4

1–2 lb raw shrimp or	*coarse salt*
scampi, with heads	*about ¼ cup fat capers*

FOR REAL MAYONNAISE

1 tbsp white-wine vinegar	*1¼ cup olive oil or 3:1 plain*
pinch of salt	*oil and extra virgin*
2 large yolks (plus 1 egg	*olive oil*
white in a blender)	*freshly ground black pepper*

First make the mayonnaise. Put the vinegar and salt in a bowl (or blender or food processor). Add the egg yolks to the bowl (use 1 whole egg plus 1 yolk in a blender) and beat (or blend) to a cream.

Add the oil (not extra virgin) drop by drop, if working with a beater, until the mixture emulsifies. Add more oil in larger quantities as the mayonnaise thickens, until it is all absorbed. Add the extra virgin oil last, if using. Taste and correct the seasonings.

This mayonnaise is thick, yellow and viscous, unlike bottled mayonnaise. It can be thinned with 1½–3 tablespoons of boiling water if it is to be kept.

Cook the shellfish in a large pan of salted water. Big scampi with heads on (where 10–12 of them weigh 2 lb) will need about 6 minutes. Big deep-water shrimp need about 3 minutes and smaller shrimp 2 minutes. Cook little shrimps in batches – just plunging them in and out for a minute. Drain and serve in a big dish, scattered with coarse salt.

Crush the capers with the back of a spoon, stir into the mayonnaise, and pile into a bowl. Provide plates for the shells, and napkins, if the shellfish are still hot.

Balearic Garden Salad

—— o ——

TREMPÓ

This pretty, fresh salad includes fruit and the local capers, which grow on the Balearic hillsides and are sold pickled to the whole of Spain.

SERVES 4

3 firm tomatoes, sliced in rings
3 tbsp olive oil
2 tbsp vinegar
pinch of salt
freshly ground black pepper
1 ripe pear, peeled, cored and sliced
1 apple, cored and sliced

2 green peppers, seeded, and sliced in rings
2 spring onions, chopped
small bunch of purslane or watercress tips
½ ship's biscuit or 2 water biscuits
3 tbsp capers

Line a big plate or shallow salad bowl with the tomato slices. Beat together the oil, vinegar, salt and black pepper in a bowl and put the pear and apple slices into this as they are ready, turning to coat them (otherwise they will discolour). Arrange these over the tomatoes.

Arrange the pepper rings on top and sprinkle with the white and green of the spring onions. Tuck bunches of purslane or watercress round the plate and in between the tomato. Dot with pieces of crumbled biscuit and capers and sprinkle with the remaining vinaigrette.

Layered Aubergine, Potato and Tomato Casserole

—— o ——

TUMBET

Aubergine dishes in the Mediterranean date from the time of the Moors. This one must have been updated when tomatoes, peppers and potatoes were introduced from America. It is typical of the rather solid soups and vegetable dishes of the islands, made in the earthenware *greixonera*.

SERVES 6

2 medium aubergines
salt and freshly ground black pepper
9 small potatoes, peeled and sliced
2 large Spanish onions, chopped
6 tbsp olive oil
2 garlic cloves, finely chopped

2 big green peppers, seeded and sliced
1 big red pepper, seeded and sliced
9–10 tbsp chopped parsley
3 × 400-g (14-oz) cans tomatoes
2 tsp paprika
3 tbsp red wine vinegar

122

Slice the aubergine very thinly, lay the slices out on the draining board and sprinkle with salt. Leave to sweat for 30–40 minutes, then blot with kitchen paper. Prepare the potatoes and cook them for 15 minutes in boiling salted water. Soften the onions in 4 tablespoons of oil over a low heat, then add the garlic.

Grease an earthenware dish or casserole (about 30 cm (12 in) across and at least 8 cm (3 in) deep) with oil. Make three layers of vegetables, starting with a third of the potato slices, then the aubergine slices, then the peppers, cooked onion and garlic together with some of the pan oil, plus parsley. Add 1 can tomatoes and its juice, squeezing the tomatoes through clenched fingers to break them up well. Season with salt, pepper and the paprika and repeat until all ingredients are in. Sprinkle vinegar over the second layer and 1 tablespoon of oil over the top of the dish.

Cover with foil and bake in a preheated oven at 200°C/400°F (Gas 6) for 1 hour. Then remove the foil, turn down the heat to 170°C/325°F (Gas 3) and give it another 30–60 minutes to brown and concentrate the juices. Excellent hot or cold, this dish also reheats well.

Almond-Stuffed Pork with Sherry and Cream

○

LOMO DE CERDO ALMENDRADO

Lomo (pork loin) is a popular Spanish cut of seamless meat. I first came across this dish, though, which is stuffed through with crisp, toasted almonds, as a couple of tenderloins tied together: a cheaper but less generous alternative. To do this, split them the same way, beat them out, then sandwich together. I wondered if the English, who introduced dairy cows to the Balearic Islands, had influenced this sauce, but I suspect it is related to Arab dishes of birds simmered in milk.

SERVES 6

1¾ lb eye-of-pork loin, 6–7
  chop center loin, boned,
  skinned and all flaps
  trimmed away
salt and freshly ground black
  pepper
1 cup almonds, toasted (see
  page 101)
3 tbsp flour
1 tbsp rendered pork fat
  or butter

1 tbsp olive oil
⅓ cup fino *sherry* or
  Montilla
8 whites of green onion
  or 4 shallots, chopped
2 cups meat or chicken broth
½ cup thick cream
1–2 green onions, finely
  chopped (optional)

Cut the pork almost through horizontally. Open it like a book and season both sides well. Chop the almonds coarsely (don't overprocess if using a blender or food processor) and sprinkle the inside. Shut the meat and tie it in half a dozen places with string.

Dust the pork with seasoned flour. Heat the fat and oil in a flameproof casserole (that fits the joint neatly) and then brown the outside of the meat. Douse it with the *fino* and allow this to reduce, spooning it over the meat.

Add the green onion bottoms or shallots and fry them for a couple of minutes. Pour the broth round the base of the meat. Cover the pan tightly, first with foil then the lid, and pot roast for 1 hour.

Remove the meat and let it rest in a warm place. Boil the juices to reduce by half. Stir in the cream and warm the sauce through. It is not traditional to blend the sauce, but I do. Carve the meat and arrange the slices, overlapping on a serving platter. Pour the sauce over. If you wish, a sprinkling of finely chopped green onion tops gives it a touch of green.

Pizza with Garden Vegetables

○

COCA ENRAMADA

Quicker but more of a peasant dish than Italian pizza, *cocas* have neither tomato sauce nor cheese. They are made in Valencia and Catalonia too and, fresh from the oven, the combination of bread, vegetables and olive oil is delicious. Sometimes fresh sardines or slices of local sausage go on top, and there are sweet versions for festivals. The name means "decked with a bower."

SERVES 4—6

1 Spanish onion, finely
  chopped
6 tbsp extra virgin olive oil
2 small green bell peppers,
  seeded and chopped

1 big beefsteak tomato,
  skinned and seeded
salt and freshly ground
  black pepper

FOR THE DOUGH
(or use 1 packet pizza dough)

about ¾ cup milk
2 tbsp fresh yeast or 1½ tsp
  dried yeast
½ tsp sugar (optional)

2¼ cups strong all-purpose
  flour, plus extra for
  kneading
1 tsp salt
3 tbsp olive oil, plus extra

First make the pizza dough. Warm the milk to blood heat (test with a clean finger). Cream fresh yeast with the sugar and half the milk in a cup and leave in a warm place until the top bubbles – about 10 minutes. For dried yeast follow the packet instructions.

Strain the flour into a food processor (or big bowl) and scatter with the salt. Add the dried yeast, or yeast mixture, and oil to the bowl, and work in enough of the remaining warm milk to make a dough. If using a processor, beat for 3–4 minutes, stopping every minute to break the dough up. Or turn the dough out onto a floured surface and knead, pushing it out with the heel of one hand to a tongue shape, then folding and slapping

it into a mound again. Do this until it becomes elastic. Shape it into a ball, put into an oiled bowl, cover with a cloth, and leave in a warm place for 30 minutes.

Preheat the oven to 425°F. Meanwhile soften the onion in ¼ cup of oil.

When the dough has doubled in bulk, put it in the middle of an oiled 12-in pizza plate. Press it down with your knuckles to fit the plate with a slight rim round the outside. Oil the edges of the dough and spread the onion over the dough. Distribute the peppers and tomato over the top and season with salt and pepper. Dribble another 1 tablespoon of oil over the top. Bake for 25–30 minutes. Delicious with cold beer.

Chaplain's "Partridges"

———◦———

PERDICES DE CAPELLÁN

A dish with a false name, served to poor clerics. It does not contain partridges at all, but is in fact sausage inside a thin slice of meat. In Mallorca the rolls are stuffed with a thin slice of the exquisite local *sobrasada* sausage, which is a fine paste of paprika-flavoured raw pork. If I can get the real thing, I make the dish with veal escalopes, raw ham and white wine. If not, then I use cheap alternatives – which is in keeping with the spirit of the dish – beef, cooked ham, sausagemeat seasoned with paprika and red wine. Certainly good enough for a vicar!

SERVES 6 MODESTLY

3 thin slices of beef top rump, about 600 g (1¼ lb)	*about 1 tbsp flour*
6 slices of cooked ham	*salt and freshly ground black pepper*
250 g (9 oz) good sausagemeat	*125 ml (4 fl oz) white wine*
2 tsp sweet paprika	*sprig of oregano*
2 tbsp butter	*sprig of thyme*
1 tbsp olive oil	*125 ml (4 fl oz) meat or chicken stock, or water*
3 garlic cloves	

Cover each beef slice with cling film, beat it out with a wine bottle and cut in half. Lay a slice of ham over each slice of beef and cut the beef to fit, trimming to avoid seams, gristle, and so on. The meat slice should then be about 75 g (3 oz) – this is the size to buy for veal escalopes if you want to use them.

Work the paprika into the sausagemeat in a bowl. I can buy paprika-flavoured fresh sausages. Divide the sausagemeat between the layered meats, placing it at one end. Roll them up and stitch the end in place with a cocktail stick.

Heat the butter and oil, with the garlic cloves, in a casserole of a size to take all the rolls tightly. When the garlic cloves colour, remove them to a mortar. Dust the meat rolls with seasoned flour and put them in, stick-side down. Fry until coloured on all sides.

Add the wine and the herbs with enough stock to almost cover them. Simmer, covered, for 30 minutes (beef needs longer than veal) then remove the lid, and simmer for a few minutes more to reduce the gravy. Remove the cocktail sticks, and serve the rolls with gravy poured over them.

Colorante, *the pale yellow powder shown above, is a saffron substitute and is much cheaper than the true saffron strands.*

Sweet Cheesecake with Mint

FLAÒ

Another very old recipe, that is made all round the Mediterranean, and appears in the first cookbook printed in Spain, at the end of the 15th century. Nowadays the cheesecake is eaten in Ibiza at Easter time.

SERVES 8

4 small eggs
3 tbsp honey
150 g (5 oz) caster sugar
400 g (14 oz) soft full-fat cream cheese

15 fresh mint leaves
1 tbsp dry anis or anisette (or Pernod)
icing sugar for dusting

FOR THE PASTRY

175 g (6 oz) flour, plus extra for rolling
pinch of salt
50 g (2 oz) chilled butter, diced, plus extra for greasing

1 small egg
1 tsp dry anis or anisette (or Pernod)
1–1½ tbsp milk

First make the pastry. Sift the flour and salt into a food processor or bowl. Cut in the fat, then beat in the whole egg and anis, adding enough milk to make a dough. Pull the pastry together into a ball and chill for 15 minutes.

Heat the oven to 170°C/325°F (Gas 3) with a heavy baking sheet in it to warm. Make the filling by beating the eggs, honey and sugar together. Work in the cream cheese, mint leaves and anis.

Roll out the pastry on a floured surface. Roll it round a rolling pin and lift this over a greased flan tin of 25 cm (10 in) diameter, and fit it in. Fit the pastry into the tin. Pour in the filling, smooth the top and bake on the baking sheet for 40–50 minutes until slightly risen and golden.

Leave it to cool for 5 minutes then remove the flan ring. Chill well. You can make fancy decorations on top with more fresh mint leaves, but all it needs is a dusting with some icing sugar.

Index

A

allioli 103
anchovies
  in Salad with Three Types of Cured Fish 99
  Moorish Pickled Anchovies 19
Artichoke Puffs, Deep-Fried, with Tomato Sauce 110–11
asparagus
  in Mixed Salad from Madrid 35
  in Riverbank Bake with Young Green Vegetables 94
  White Asparagus with Two Sauces 87

B

beans
  Asturian Bean & Sausage Pot (*Fabada Asturiana*) 11, 71
  Galician Bean, Pork & Greens Soup 58
  Lima Beans with Ham, Ronda Style 20
  Tolosa Red Bean Stew 85
  Uncle Luke's Mildly Spiced Beans 49
beef
  in Asturian Bean & Sausage Pot 71
  Beef with Eggplant 54
  Beef Steaks with Anchovy-Stuffed Olives 41
  Boiled Meat Dinner from Madrid (*Cocido*) 53
  Catalan Beef Stew with Chocolate 105
  in Chaplain's "Partridges" 126
  Sliced Simmered Beef with Turnips & Carrots 73
  T-Bone Steaks with Cream & Armagnac Sauce 84
Belgian Endive and Ham Gratin 81
Breadcrumbs, Fried, with Ham & Peppers 28

C

Cheese Custards 48
Cheesecake with Mint 127
Chestnut Soup 57
chicken
  Chicken with Pounded Almond Sauce 93
  Chicken with Tomatoes, Pepper & Cumin 32
  Farmyard Chicken with Olives 21
  Pot Roast Chicken with Apples 72
  Saffron Rice with Chicken & Seafood (*Paella Valenciana*) 116
  Santander Chicken with Flavored Rice 74
Chocolate, Catalan Beef Stew with 105
clams
  Pink Santander Soup with Clams & Leeks 69
  Potatoes with Clams, Cuttlefish & Peppers 80
  in Spaghettini with Shellfish 100
cocido 53
cod, salt 11
  in Salad with Three Types of Cured Fish 99
  Salt Cod in Spicy Tomato, Bay of Biscay Way 82
Crème Brûlée Ice Cream 106
Custard Squares 67
Custards, Mild Cheese 48
Cuttlefish, Clams & Peppers 80

D

desserts
  Crème Brûlée Ice Cream 106
  Creamy Chilled Rice 24
  Crisp Custard Squares 67
  Drunken Cakes 55
  Festive Walnut Cream 85
  Iced Lemonade Sorbet 119
  Muscatel Ice Cream 23
  Schoolteacher's Hazelnut Meringues 75
  Sugared Toasts 45
  Sweet Cheesecake with Mint 127
Duck with Oranges & Olives, Seville Style 22

E

eggplants
  Beef with Eggplant 54
  Layered Eggplant, Potato & Tomato Casserole 122–3
  in Murcian Salad of Mixed Baked Vegetables 114–15
  Mushroom-Stuffed Eggplants 88
  Pickled Eggplants 36
eggs
  Baked Tomato with Ham & Egg 29
  Red Basque Pepper Omelet 78
  Scrambled Eggs with Shrimp & Spring Leaves 62
  Simmered Summer Vegetables with Eggs 38
  Spanish Potato Omelet 39
escalivada 114

F

fish & shellfish
  Biscay Bay Sole with Cream & Shellfish 83
  Catalan Mussel Soup 97
  Fish Balls in Cider Sauce 70
  Fish Stew with Red Peppers & Potatoes 83
  Flat Fish with Hazelnut & Chili Sauce 101
  Fresh Shrimp with Caper Mayonnaise 121
  Grey Mullet Baked with Saffron & Potatoes 112–13
  Little Fried Pies with Tuna & Tomato 109
  Mixed Fish & Shellfish Stew 66
  Mixed Fish Stew with Garlic Sauce 102–3
  Moorish Pickled Anchovies 19
  Mussel Pancakes 60
  Pink Santander Soup with Clams & Leeks 69
  Pork with Mussels 104–5
  Potato & Fish Soup with Vinegar 16
  Potatoes with Cuttlefish, Clams & Peppers 80–1
  Riverbank Hake with Young Green Vegetables 94
  Saffron Rice with Chicken & Seafood (*Paella Valenciana*) 116
  St James's Scallops 59
  Salad with Three Types of Cured Fish 99
  Salt Cod in Spicy Tomato, Bay of Biscay Way 82
  Scrambled Eggs with Shrimp & Spring Leaves 62
  Skate with Peas & Potatoes in Paprika Sauce 63
  Spaghettini with Shellfish 100–1
  Stock 16
  Trout in Red Wine 92

G

garbanzo beans
  in Beef with Eggplant 54
  in Boiled Meat Dinner 53
  Garbanzo Beans with Spinach 41
Garlic & Bread Soup, Granny's 27
Gazpacho Soup 15

H

Hake with Young Green Vegetables 94
ham
  Baked Tomatoes with Ham & Egg 29
  Belgian Endive & Ham Gratin 81
  in Chaplain's "Partridges" 126
  Fried Breadcrumbs with Ham & Peppers 28
  Lima Beans with Ham, Ronda Style 20
Hazelnut Macaroons, Schoolteacher's 75

I

ice creams
  Crème Brûlée 106
  Muscatel 23
Iced Lemonade Sorbet 119

K

Kidneys in Sherry 18

L

lamb
  Fried Lamb with Lemon Juice 50
  Fried Lamb with Paprika & Vinegar 31
  Spicy Lamb with Peppers 93
Lentils, Perfect Plain 50
Lima Beans with Ham 20
Liver in Red Wine Sauce 33

M

Mayonnaise 121
Meatballs with Saffron 36
Mixed Spring Vegetable Pot 91
Moorish Kebabs, Small Spicy 16
Moorish Pickled Anchovies 19
Muscatel Ice Cream 23
Mushroom-Stuffed Eggplants 88
Mushrooms, Well-Seasoned 89
mussels
  Catalan Mussel Soup 97
  Mussel Pancakes 60
  Pork with Mussels 104–5
  in Saffron Rice with Chicken and Seafood (*Paella Valenciana*) 116
  in Spaghettini with Shellfish 100–1

P

Paella Valenciana 116
Partridges in Wine with New Potatoes 42
Peppers, Baked, with Rice & Meat Stuffing 111
picada 103
Pies, Little Fried, with Tuna & Tomatoes 109
Pizza with Garden Vegetables 124–5
pork
  Almond-Stuffed Pork with Sherry & Cream 124
  in Asturian Bean & Sausage Pot 71
  in Boiled Meat Dinner from Madrid 53
  Galician Bean, Pork & Greens Soup 50
  Meatballs with Saffron 36
  Pork Chops with Capers & Peppers 118
  Pork with Mussels 104–5
  Rice with Pork & Spinach 119
  in Small Spicy Moorish Kebabs 16
  Tolosa Red Bean Stew with Pork 85
potatoes
  Potato & Fish Soup with Vinegar 16
  Potatoes with Cuttlefish, Clams & Peppers 80–1
  Potatoes Made Special 47
  Potatoes in Spicy Tomato Sauce 98
  Skate with Peas & Potatoes in Paprika Sauce 63
  Spanish Potato Omelet 39

Q

Quail, Braised, with Muscatel Grapes 94–5
Quails in Knapsacks 52

R

Rabbit & Onion Pie 64
Rabbit with Saffron & Aromatics 44
rice
  Baked Peppers with Rice & Meat Stuffing 111
  Creamy Chilled Rice 24
  Rice with Fish & Vegetables 115
  Rice with Pork & Spinach 119
  Saffron Rice with Chicken & Seafood (*Paella Valenciana*) 116
  Santander Chicken with Flavored Rice 74
Romesco Sauce 101
Roquefort Dressing 79

S

salads
  Baked Salad of Red Peppers & Tomato 90
  Balearic Garden Salad 122
  Mixed Salad from Madrid 35
  Murcian Salad of Mixed Baked Vegetables 114–15
  Orange Salad with Garlic & Red Wine 48
  Salad with Roquefort Dressing 79
  Salad with Three Types of Cured Fish 99
Scallops, St James's 59
shellfish, *see* fish & shellfish
shrimp
  Fresh Shrimp with Caper Mayonnaise 121
  in Mixed Fish & Shellfish Stew 100
  in Mixed Fish Stew with Garlic Sauce 102–3
  Overcoated Shrimp 77
  Scrambled Eggs with Shrimp & Spring Leaves 62
  in Spaghettini with Shellfish 100–1
Simmered Summer Vegetables with Eggs 38
Skate with Peas & Potatoes in Paprika Sauce 63
Sole, Biscay Bay, with Cream & Shellfish 83
soups
  Catalan Mussel Soup 97
  Creamy Chestnut Soup 57
  Galician Bean, Pork & Greens Soup 58
  Granny's Garlic & Bread Soup 27
  Icy Red Gazpacho 15
  Pink Santander Soup with Clams & Leeks 69
  Potato & Fish Soup with Vinegar 16
Spaghettini with Shellfish 100
Sugared Toasts 45

T

tapas
  Kidneys in Sherry 18
  Mussel Pancakes 60
  Overcoated Shrimp 77
  Potatoes in Spicy Tomato Sauce 98
  Small Spicy Moorish Kebabs 16
  Spanish Potato Omelet 39
Tomatoes, Baked, with Ham & Eggs 29
Trout in Red Wine 92
tuna
  in Fish Stew with Red Peppers & Potatoes 83
  in Granny's Garlic & Bread Soup 27
  in Salad with Three Types of Cured Fish 99
  Little Fried Pies with Tuna & Tomato 109
  in Mixed Salad from Madrid 35

V

vinaigrette 35

W

Walnut Cream, Festive 85

Z

Zucchini and Onion Hash 112